THE
MILLIONAIRE

FATHER

...because
every child
deserves a
great father!

JEFFREY M. REITZEL

FOGHORN
PUBLISHERS
"Of Making Many Books There Is No End..."

The Millionaire Father—2009

ISBN-10: 1-934466-25-5
ISBN-13: 978-1-934466-25-4

Printed in the United States of America
© 2009 by Jeff Reitzel

For more information about Jeff Reitzel, his forthcoming books
and motivational seminars go to:
www.themillionairefather.com

Foghorn Publishers
P.O. Box 8286
Manchester, CT 06040-0286
860-216-5622

foghornpublisher@aol.com
www.foghornpublisher.com

DEDICATION

This book is dedicated to my beautiful wife Penny, my 2 sons Joshua and Lucas, and my parents Jim and Sharon Reitzel. None of this would be possible without them. They have made me the Millionaire Father that I am today.

Thanks for all your love and support!

TABLE OF CONTENTS

INTRODUCTION

This book was written with the sole purpose of expressing to all dads that every child deserves a great father, and that means somebody who is around… OFTEN! Children are a whole lot different than adults. At times, adults measure love by how much you spend on them. Your children measure love by the amount of time you spend with them, not by the amount you spend on them. With the importance our society places on monetary value, it's not too surprising that most people expect all things to have a dollar price connected to it.

However, love from your children cannot be bought! The bond that you share will always exist on a subconscious level, the deepest level ever. So it is imperative that you express your love directly and exemplify it daily through your actions. The one thing about children is that they almost instinctively know when your love is genuinely there. Unfortunately, your love can't be there too often when you aren't there.

The average father works a full-time job, which requires him to work 40 hours or more each week. With this grueling schedule, he barely spends an hour and a half with their children a day. There are 24 hours in each day, yet the average father gives less than ten-percent of their time to their children. Think about it, sitting down to have dinner with your family will not take too much time out of your schedule, neither will casually talking with them about what happened in school for a quick ten or fifteen minutes after they get home. However, all of these things-to-do quickly add up, zapping away the precious time you already have so little of.

Time then becomes your most precious and coveted commodity. In the same way that people often complain about not having enough money, people often complain about not having enough time. Unfortunately, when you don't seem to have enough time, you begin to devote your life to things that inevitably take more of your time away. Interestingly though, the more time you spend with your children, something almost magical happens—you will want to spend more time with them. You will want to do whatever it takes to do things with them.

Providing for your child is important. However, nothing can replace spending quality time with your child. Children need proper guidance and care so that they can mature into prosperous and successful adults. This kind of care can only come from one-on-one contact with a loving parent. The problems are conflicting and competing commitments. On one hand you have a dad who does absolutely nothing to provide for his child, yet has all the time in the world to spend with his child, since he is doing absolutely nothing in life.

Then you have the guy who makes loads of money and gives his child every material desire, but barely knows what his child even looks like since he is away from home ninety percent of the time. It is obvious money is important. Everyone not only needs it to survive, but some also need it to place themselves at a higher level in society. There must be balance though. There are some folks that have hundreds of millions of dollars yet don't understand the value of spending a few hours with their children: mentoring them, instructing them and yes of course, just having fun with them.

So busy accumulating more, they forget about the real meaning of family and fathering. They get seduced into a self-defeating cycle of "more, more, more," and "I just can't get enough." Paying your bills and supplying food for the house are necessary. But at what expense do you pay to continue to work hard for more stuff? Just accept the fact that there will always be someone with more money and more success; the issue is accepting this fact and learning how to use what you already have and make it grow.

Providing for your family should be your major priority and that isn't too hard to do, with a little hard work. Setting your family up for a lifetime of comfort, even after you're gone, doesn't require as much hard work as it only requires literal and fiscal toughness. Some men falsely believe that when they are successful and have social status that their children will be more proud of them. Sasha and Malia, President Barack Obama's children, love him, but not because he is the President of the United States, or a former U.S. Senator for that matter. They love him because of the time that he intentionally invests in each of them.

You could have the most basic and elementary job, and even the dirtiest, and guess what, your children will still find admirable qualities in you if you spend time with them. You don't have to be or have the income of Sean "Puffy" Combs, Donald Trump, Bill Gates or Wayne Gretzky to be honored by your child. In your child's eye, you are far more important than they could ever be, because they are not "daddy." Those important rich men don't spend the kind of quality time with them that you do. That makes all the difference in the world.

Being a dad of six years, I find fathering as the most incredible experience of my life. I wouldn't exchange it for the world. I feel obligated though and almost compelled to help my fellow fathers to understand how to get out of the rat race, the race that never ends. My goal is to expose fathers to the path, instructing them step-by-step on the "how-tos" of earning more money, without adding more hours to their existing work schedule. On the other hand, I'm here to help the father, who already has plenty of money, understand how to enjoy what he has and learn to embrace great opportunities, like spending memorable moments with their child.

The father that has enough but doesn't realize it yet can be shown a path to discover this, so that he won't have to continually chase after wealth while overlooking the greatest wealth right in his home. By the time I had reached my late twenties, I was fortunate enough to be a millionaire. At this period of time, most adults are still deciding on what career they'd like to have. Not having to worry about wealth accumulation, I was able to focus most of my quality time on my family, which is the dwelling place of true prosperity.

You may be wondering why I am even sharing this with you. The number one reason for sharing my knowledge is that I want to be able to make a difference in people's lives financially, which in turn will make a difference in their personal lives. Many people don't realize the impact that financial security has on the emotional stability and family growth. Consider me your mentor. All true mentors in life help to shorten the distance for their mentees.

Being an avid sports fan, I am always intrigued by watching great teams win. What I have come to discover is that the greatest players are not great solely based on their sports ability, but rather because they know what moves to make, and more importantly, when to make them. That is essentially what I am here to do. I've already been there and made the moves, both good and bad ones, creating wealth and losing it all. Through my life's ups and downs and then finally becoming solidly focused on purpose, I can show you how to become The Millionaire Father.

The Millionaire Father is not as much about money as it is creating options in life. The difference between the poor and the rich really boils down to that one word—"options." The rich generally have far more options than the not so rich. Whichever group you fall into, I'm here to give you options. I truly hope this book influences you enough for you to desire change in your life and realize that the money is always available. You just need to know the right moves to win at the money game. After I show you those, just promise to win in life at something greater than money—being a great dad!

Jeff Reitzel
The Millionaire Father—2009

1

IS MONEY LOOKING FOR YOU?

Have you ever wondered why some people succeed at such a high level, personally or financially, and others just go from day to day with no positive changes in their life? In my experience, people that succeed at the highest levels all have bigger purposes or "Why's" that drive them on a daily basis. It is the "Why's" in life that makes the difference between success and failure. The people that live their life with intentional purpose tend to have money chasing them, since money never pursues anyone in life that does not have a plan in place.

These people maintain and pursue the goals and aspirations that they not only want to achieve, but their goals also inspire them to be far more focused in life. It is concentrated focus that always yields amazing results. What are your "Big Why's" or purposes and goals for being on this earth? The answer to that question is crucial to your development, growth and of course, your financial well being. Is your goal to feed the hungry in Africa or even in your home city? Is it to ensure that your family never struggles financially?

Maybe your goal is to buy a big house or drive a luxury car. Perhaps you have those other things, yet you would love to spend more time with your family and the people you love the most. Do you sometimes feel that the only reason you were placed on this earth is to work every day and struggle to make a living, being barely able to provide for yourself and for your family? One thing that you may have overlooked is that the smallest aspects of your life can lift you beyond this miserable feeling of desperation.

Right now, I want you to think of some "Why's" but don't judge whether or not they are good or bad, big or small; just consider them in your mind. For example, my "Big Why's" and purposes on this earth are to be a great father, loving husband and a strong business leader, empowering others to succeed while serving my community to the best of my ability. These various roles represent the most important parts of me. It is what I am designed to manifest in life, to become all that I am supposed to be.

 *You must intend to succeed.*

This is somewhat of a mission statement for my life that I subconsciously rehearse in my mind on a daily basis. It's a part of the working system in place that helps to keep me wholly focused when I am tempted to get off course. You, too, should develop a working, written mission statement for your life, rather than go from day to day and simply expect things to happen, just because. Things in life don't work that way. You must intend to succeed. And on top of that, you must have a direction in which you are going and also a goal that you are striving for.

An archer never shoots arrows in the air; he or she always has a target. My target, my aspirations may be totally different than yours. That's perfectly fine because we are all different. This book is not about getting you to think like me. It's all about getting you to tap into your greatest potential so that you can become the kind of parent that your children deserve. Your target may shift as you meet the different needs in your life at certain points of time. The main goal in your life may change as you grow older or as your environment evolves around you and that's okay. Even when things are changing, your family will always be rooted within you.

What I need to do in life and why I need to do it is very clear to me, making my job on this earth much easier. They are the motivation to every financial move that I make within my career; they all lead to the ultimate goal of bettering the lives of those around me. When you are very clear as to what your purpose is, waking up in the morning becomes an easy task, as you are excited about every day. Yes, it is even possible to be excited about going to work! When money knows where you are and why you want it, it will find you. Remember that.

 *Money is Good for the good it can do.*

People tend to falsely ascribe to the concept that money looks for you when you are in the worst state of affairs. That simply isn't true. Money runs away from people in trouble. Money comes for one reason and one reason only; to solve problems. Money is a solution. Money helps me to be a better father, husband, business leader and contributor to my community.

Without it, I couldn't do nearly as much as I do. Contribution is extremely important to me; it is the ultimate purpose for my existence. Money helps me to make contributing a reality. The amount of money waiting to be yours is limitless, as long as it is looking for you to take advantage of it. Here is the key: Knowing why you want financial success is crucial in creating wealth. If you don't know why, then money isn't obligated to show up.

What Good Is Money?

What good is money? Money is only good for the good that it can do, nothing more and nothing less. The other day I was driving and saw what appeared to be a very poor woman. She was somewhere around 70-years-old, getting ready to walk into a local soup kitchen. When I saw her, I didn't judge her; neither did I try to reason why she was in this situation. In fact, just seeing her and feeling empathy for her situation became a great motivator for me to continue doing what I am doing for multiple reasons.

First and foremost, I wanted to make sure I don't end up in a situation similar to hers. There is something very strange about life. Nobody ever thinks that they could end up in such a dire place. In life, you just never know. I guess that's one of many reasons to be very thankful. It would be really easy to criticize this woman for being in such a desperate situation, but there are far too many factors to consider when dealing with situations like these than to just conclude that she did something wrong. For me, it would be hard to believe that this woman would have ever thought she would be in this situation.

It probably never crossed her mind that one day she would rely solely on the help of others to provide for herself. Nobody is completely secure in his or her position, especially in the economy we exist in today. However, if you take the proper precautions and maintain a positive attitude about financial security that will definitely help. Even though I am a millionaire with a lot of money at my disposal, it could be gone in a day through one business mistake. Where would I be then? Where would my family be?

In life you have to take everything into account. You have to look at the bigger picture. One other thing that this woman's situation reminded me of was the fact that my family, and others that are close to me, will eventually age. We all will get old at some point; even the budding teenager that thinks that life is endless will get old eventually. I would never want to see anyone fall into that situation in their golden years, when they should relaxing from all of their years of hard labor.

You have to look at the bigger picture.

Even after I am long gone from this earth, I would still like to prevent this kind of situation from happening to anyone in my family. At times, old age can prohibit the body and the mind from being as useful as it was in its earlier years. However, this woman did not just affect me in terms of my life and the life of my family; I also saw her as a fellow human being in great need of help—help that I could provide if I was willing.

The more money I obtained, the more I would be able to give away, especially to places that needed it the most (like the soup kitchen she was going into). Where did the food that fed these people in need come from? Thankfully, there are many people who have a little money to spare in order to provide for those that cannot do so for themselves. Just think about it, if I had a lot of money to spare, I would be able to go above and beyond my present giving to help provide the physical sustenance to people in need of assistance.

The community is the basis for a home and strong families. So the more built up it is, the more it will produce. I want my children to grow up in the best possible environment, so giving my money to the community makes perfect sense. Perhaps I'd also be able to inspire this woman and give her hope, reminding her that she was not put on this earth to live in such a deprived position but to rise above it.

Many people downplay the benefits and importance of money. Don't believe the lie!

The sad thing is this woman only represented one of many in need; those that did not realize early on that money was looking for them and that it was within their grasp to be as financially successful as I am. So you want to know what good money is? Well, money is good for the purpose of changing people's bad situations into better ones. For this woman, money meant that she was able to eat a meal at the soup kitchen, which someone's finances obviously provided for. Money could also provide for this woman to get the necessary knowledge to help her understand how to maintain financial freedom.

Money helps our children to get an education. It helps people to have quality healthcare. Money helps people to be able to keep the jobs they have. Without money, businesses go out of business all of the time. So it is no secret that money does a whole lot of good. That's what's good about money. There are so many people that try to downplay the great benefits of money and make it seem as if it's not all that important. Don't believe the lie!

Money is good, and if you desire to be the kind of father that not only wants to leave a legacy to his children, but also wants to spend quality time with them, you will have to become comfortable with the concept that money is a good idea. Recently, I visited one of my clients that I have worked with for ten years. For the sake of anonymity, we will call my client Stan. Stan used to occasionally ask me to come over and join him for coffee. We would do this a couple times a year. However, at this particular meeting he pulled out plans for two different retirement facilities in Florida that he was considering.

One of the facilities was $4,000.00 a month and the other was $6,000.00 a month and he asked me which one I would pick. Now, I was 29-years-old at the time and had only visited one or two retirement homes in my life so I knew little to nothing about what he should look for. I said, "Stan, which one do you like the best?" He replied option B, the one that costs $6,000.00 a month. Then my advice was to go with that one. Stan looked at me and said, "It is $2,000.00 more a month than the first one." So I agreed he should go with the first one, since it was far less expensive.

He replied that he didn't like the first one as it didn't provide the same services and wasn't as nice of a facility. I replied, "Stan, you have done a great job creating wealth for your family, you have been great dedicating your time and money to your community and you are also now at the stage where $2,000.00 a month isn't going to have a big impact on your overall cash flow or net worth; in my opinion it is time to enjoy what you have built." Wow, this guy had choices. He had options, unlike the older lady at the soup kitchen. Well actually, she had options also, but was just unaware of them.

Wouldn't we all like to be in a place where we can make decisions not based on the cost? This is possible for everyone and as you continue reading, I am going to show you how to do just that. Not only was Stan so financially successful that he could sleep easy on his decision to spend such a great amount of money, he had also thoroughly enjoyed the process in which he had created his wealth. Financial prosperity does not necessarily mean being able to spend large amounts of money at a whim's notice, but rather it signifies that you are comfortable and secure with your monetary decisions.

Financial prosperity... signifies that you are comfortable and secure with your monetary decisions.

The journey to this kind of comfort does not have to be one filled with struggle and hours and hours of work; it can be pleasurable, mentally, physically and spiritually satisfying. I truly believe that before you move forward with this book or in your financial journey, you need to start coming up with some "Why's." Once these are laid out, much of the work you will have to do to reach your financial goals will seem more like fun and an exciting challenge, rather than actual labor. I've never felt like it was a drag to go to work.

Honestly, I have a clear passion for what I do in my profession. This is because I have great purpose behind what I do. I will confess that when I started my wealth-building path I didn't know what the true reason was; today I understand fully that it was to become the Millionaire Father that I am today! Everybody's process is different. I am here as a coach to give you options to choose from and to help you to tailor make a plan that will fit what's best for you, eventually propelling you more rapidly toward your goal.

How To Create Why's

Let me start of by making a disclosure. I cannot give you desire, and neither can I tell you what is important to you. You have to intrinsically know those things for yourself. As a coach, I am obligated only to help you to become aware of some of the things, some of the greatness lying dormant within you that you may have been overlooking for so many years. Everybody has greatness within them. Most people however just don't recognize it. What you do not recognize you cannot capitalize on. Now I realize that every soul in the universe will not become a millionaire. But that doesn't mean that you won't. You will become a millionaire only when your why becomes absolutely urgent. So let's get clear on the "Why's."

Personal Steps To Creating Your Why

First, think about the areas where you are lacking happiness in your life. Perhaps it isn't financially, but morally, spiritually or in your relationships—especially with your family. Are you lacking in quality time with your children, pleasurable moments with your family or a deep relationship with your wife? Where do these problems stem from? Obviously, as a father and husband, you enjoy the positions that you are currently filling. So if you'd like to better your relationship with your family, perhaps your "Why" should simply be the fact that you want to make them happy and feel secure, loved and provided for.

Of course, it is possible that you are lacking financially. In an uncertain economy, it's not hard to find yourself settling for a minimum wage job and working overtime just to pay the bills. Not having money can stress your mind and consume your being; it can get you totally out of balance emotionally. So having money should be a must for the person who desperately needs it. Survival leans on money, which is why many people become so jaded about the idea of money. However, making money should never be your "Why" but the means to manifesting it. Your why could sound like this, "I need to make more money so that I can _____." That blank spot represents your why in life once you fill in the blank. Again this will be different for everyone.

 *The things that bring you the most joy in life should always be considered your "Why's"...*

Also, your "Why" should be something that you enjoy, something that excites you. Maybe you never wanted to have a career in the business world but desired deeply, when you were a child or even young adult, to be involved in something else, maybe the arts, music, to work in restaurants, create architectural renderings, or write books. Then, your "Why" should be being able to pursue these endeavors, perhaps not as a career now, but definitely as side interests or hobbies. The things that bring you the most joy in life should always be considered your "Why's" because those are the things that give you motivation; they are what help you to get out of bed in the morning. They add to the enrichment of your life.

Your "Why" may not have anything to do with what you're good at either. You could be good at making money, but that doesn't mean that's the only reason why you are on this earth. Like I've said before, money is disposable, interchangeable and available but you are not. You are indispensable to your family because no one can replace your influence on your children or your support for your family. The ideals that you are going to impart to your children are yours; the love that you give to your family is only yours as well. What you can contribute to society, through your money, is also irreplaceable.

Since you are not replaceable, especially to your family, that means that we need more of you; your family needs more of you. So the following chapters will show you in a rather detailed way exactly how to get more of yourself back. It begins with discovering your "Why." If you haven't felt as if you have pinned down exactly what your "Why" is, don't worry about it. Just keep reading and I believe that as you do, much of what you don't know right at this moment will suddenly begin to unfold.

CHAPTER SUMMARY

- People who succeed at the highest levels all have bigger purposes or "why's."

- Start off by thinking of some "why's" without judging whether or not they are good or bad.

- You must intend to exceed.

- Money is good for the good it can do.

- When you are very clear as to what your purpose is, you are excited about every day.

- The more money I obtain, the more I'm able to give away.

2

BELIEVING THAT YOU CAN

One of the most difficult challenges to becoming entirely wealthy does not so much depend on the physical ability of a person, but rather the mental capacity of that person to realize deep within that they can do it. This limiting mindset of believing that becoming wealthy is impossible is perhaps one of the most difficult steps for people to overcome on the path to financial freedom. It is so important that you believe you can do it, you are worth it and that you deserve to have much more in life—because you do! Let me repeat that, you can do it, you are worth it and you deserve to have anything that you desire.

Okay then, you have now been given permission to succeed. Please don't believe that I needed to give you this permission, because the ability to succeed is already within you, waiting to be tapped into. Perhaps throughout the entire course of your life, no one has actually told you that the dream of financial freedom was possible, or that you should even go after wealth. From personal experiences, I am informing you that it is possible for anyone to achieve financial prosperity. At the start of this book, I mentioned that very few of us grew up in environments that encouraged wealth creation.

Added to that, most people are not financially literate, so it is not only uncomfortable for some people to talk about money, most people don't even know the language. For those who grew up in poor or just below middle class families, money wasn't freely discussed, and when it was, it always carried a negative connotation with it. Everyone has heard sayings like, "Money is the root of all evil," "Money doesn't grow on trees," "Do you think I'm made of money?" and so on. We were constantly berated as children for being wasteful or greedy, even if our parents were well off and had stable, profitable jobs.

 Imagine what your life would be like if you always heard phrases that helped to reinforce all of the positive aspects of money.

Anytime we wanted to splurge on something really indulgent, we were quickly reminded that there were children in worse conditions than ours, making our desires for the newest toys or fashions seemingly superficial and selfish. How much would it have changed your perspective about money if you heard growing up, "Money can grow on trees, so go and plant some money seeds," "Great things can be done with money" or better yet, "You must always respect money." Imagine what your life would be like if you always heard phrases that helped to reinforce all of the positive aspects of money.

As adults our outlook would be so different in the most positive sense, that we would have a newfound determination to obtain money, realizing its potential to do so much good. Money must always be respected for the good it can do. What you respect will reproduce itself in greater magnitude. What you fail to respect, you will loose. Contrary to all of the negative things you hear on the news and read in the newspaper, there is an abundance of money in this world and you can have whatever portion of it that you desire. Before you can seize your rightful portion in life, you must first rid yourself of all the limiting beliefs that caused you to think the way you do. You must become reconditioned.

Misunderstandings about Money

There are many common misunderstandings about money that cause us to not have it. I believe one reason people don't have money is the way their mind has been conditioned over the years to believe that it is a bad thing. We relate wealth to power and power to corruption, creating a chain effect for our negative feelings. I often see couples earning high six-figure incomes but unable to make the minimum payments on their credit cards. In order for people to feel they are living morally or as good people, they will make sure they spend or get rid of whatever amount of money they have; after all money is the root of all evil, isn't it?

 *Having lots of money doesn't change you. It reveals who you really are.*

Do you know someone that was broke when they earned $20,000 a year and now make $100,000 a year, but are still broke? Having money is not as much about earning more money than it is about understanding how money works. Maintaining your wealth has to do with how you view money, how you understand it. Some people cannot wrap their minds around the fact that bringing in money doesn't necessarily mean keeping it, or that no matter how much money they make they can still find themselves in poverty. Part of the reason why money has adopted such a negative connotation is that people spend it unwisely and spontaneously on useless goods. Many people aspire to be like celebrities, able to afford $2,000 a night hotel rooms, yachts and shopping sprees on a regular basis but we must realize that money does run out eventually, especially when you wastefully splurge.

Of course there will always be money available in the world for us to obtain, but why not keep the money that we make along the way? The true "evil" may not be limited to hoarding money but spending it unwisely and without caution. Wealth is not reserved for the people with high incomes. Just because people receive higher paychecks it does not mean that they have done more work than the average person or that they deserve the money just because of the job they hold. Actually, if you look at many wealthy people, they have what some might consider "mid-level jobs" with average incomes.

Their secret to building wealth is that they have become good at managing what they have, investing their money wisely. If you don't know much about investing, at first it may be a bit difficult to know exactly where you should start. People are so concerned with keeping the money they have, it makes them nervous to entrust it to others. However, if done properly, this is a good way to start building wealth from the money you already have. Despite what negative things you have heard about investing, you must embrace the truth: Money only multiplies after it's been invested.

You will not become wealthy unless you invest. Truthfully, there are so many different kinds of investments; I'm not necessarily selling one over the other. Due to my profession, it's quite natural for me to encourage you to invest in real estate, only because I have personally benefitted from this type of invest-ment and have taught thousands of people how to do the same. But there are other investments, which we will touch upon, later in the book, such as stocks, land and even intellectual prop-erty. For now just understand that you must invest and reinvest your income in order to grow your portfolio.

 *The bottom line is this: everybody is investing in something.*

You can earn hundreds of thousands of dollars and still struggle to make ends meet. So whatever amount of money you make, begin to invest in areas that will bring back a return. The bottom line is this: everybody is investing in something. The question is, whether or not you'll get a financial return. Some people are content with the return of having other people look at them and say, "That guy must be really cool, because he wears the nicest clothes, and drives the fanciest cars."

What they don't know is that you still owe the credit card for the clothes that you charged, and that you don't even have gas money for your fancy car. For this kind of guy, the return is having people think well of them. For me, I want the kind of return that will make my children speak well of me, the kind that equals being able to take great care of them and eventually take care of myself when I'm unable to work any longer.

One example I often use in my teachings to demonstrate this are the Real Estate Investor Club meetings I used to attend years ago. When I first joined, I would sit beside people that looked like they just finished working for the day at the local factory or maybe as a landscaper or repairperson. These are jobs that society wouldn't link with someone that would be wealthy, definitely not the kinds of careers that would lead to the wealth. We sometimes picture wealthy people in Brioni and Oxford suits and driving Lamborghinis; at least that's what I thought.

Those were the kinds of people I expected to show up at these Real Estate Investors meetings. At this point in my life and career, I know all too well that looks can be very deceiving. Back then; I used to think that the person in the $100,000 car and million-dollar house had the most money because they had had the outward show. I am not suggesting that none of the people who drive around in fancy luxury cars and wear fine clothing are broke. I'm only saying that those things should not be the only or even the main determining factor to decide a person's wealth status.

There are some people who don't wear suits at all, and drive around in the most pitiful cars ever, yet have a strong financial portfolio. So then, income is not the end-all in becoming wealthy. I couldn't emphasize this point enough. It's not how much you make but rather what you do with what you make that makes all the difference in your financial future. Many high-income earners that I know personally have high salaries but almost nothing in the way of net worth. These factory workers, landscapers or repair people could easily resent what they have to do to get money; in turn, making them resent money as well. But instead they choose to take what they have and place it in an arena that will work for them, even when they aren't working.

Don't Bear a Grudge Against Money

Okay then, there are many people who hold limiting beliefs about money, and of course how you think about money will definitely determine whether or not you'll actually have money. But one of the things that I want to help you with is knowing how to focus on the right things so that you won't resent money. For the Millionaire Father, money is a primary tool that helps us to optimally fulfill our function as dads. Money helps you to be better providers, betters lovers to your spouses (if you have one), and money helps you to create the right kind of environment for you and your child to spend quality time.

So those are the benefits, just a few though, of what having more money can do for you. So even if you are working in a job you don't really like right now, don't become resentful about money. And yes, this kind of thing happens all of the time, people become so resentful about money having to work like a dog to earn it, and then the little that you have gets taken away by creditors. This can lead to a negative outlook on wealth. You'll begin to resent the fact that money seems so evasive and hard to get. You'll resent the time and energy that you dedicate only to exchange for just a few pieces of paper. That isn't life, that's survival. And all of us were put on this earth to do more than simply survive.

 *And all of us were put on this earth to do more than simply survive.*

So then, when you look at money in its proper context you will realize that money was designed to be manipulated by its user, not the other way around. We must learn how to manipulate money to our advantage, in the same way that these average workers did at the Real Estate Investors workshops. It doesn't take an enormous amount of money to increase your present financial status. However, it does take the right kind of attitude, an attitude of gratefulness for what you already have. This may sound like old principles, and they are. These principles have lasted for many centuries.

What you value and honor will increase in your life. What you do not value will quickly slip away from your embrace. Another principle lies within the fact that you must embrace the idea of having more money with a heart of gratitude. You cannot despise your present state. Deep within you must know that your financial state will change for the better in time. Don't despise where you are right now, because where you are now is the much-needed springboard to get you where you truly desire to be.

A Million Dollar House On An Average Income

Some time ago, I received a call from a client who wanted me to come over and discuss their financing options. They didn't give me any upfront information about their situation, so I was pretty clueless as to what they wanted to talk about. When I turned onto the client's street, I noticed how nice the houses in this neighborhood were, definitely an upscale neighborhood. His house was valued at somewhere in between $900,000.00 to nearly one million dollars. For most people that's a whole lot of money. When I rang the doorbell, a woman answered the door, decked with glistening diamond matching jewelry worth far more than my car.

She had the appearance of the perfect homemaker. Inside I noticed that the living room and dining room did not have furniture in them. In the kitchen there was only a fold-up card table to sit at. Her husband came in, with his diamond watch and designer suit to join us in a preliminary word warm up.

Quickly I began to discover why I was there. The house that they had lived in for five years had no furniture because they couldn't afford furniture, and neither could they afford the house. Maybe you might be wondering, "How is possible to own a million dollar house and not be able to afford a couch?" Great question! Let me fill you in.

The husband was a factory worker and only earned $65,000 per year, while his wife, a homemaker had no income at all. Honestly I was somewhat perplexed as to how they could afford a million dollar home on one single low salary. Looking at their financials I thought the next thing we were going to dis- cuss was strategies for selling their home and transitioning into something that was more affordable. I was totally mistaken. They had a $500,000 mortgage on the home and an additional $250,000 in consumer debt.

 *"How is possible to own a million dollar house and not be able to afford a couch?" Great question! Let me fill you in.*

Somehow they had managed to finagle paperwork, tricking the mortgage lenders into thinking that they would be able to pay off such a large amount of money. They wanted me to secure a new mortgage that would pay off the existing $750,000 of total debt wrapping the total amount into one mortgage. This would, in turn, free up the $250,000 to become available, usable credit that they could then tap into using to finance their lavish lifestyle for at least another five years. In five years, they were hoping that property values would skyrocket and then they could repeat the process all over again.

This was their master plan and I wasn't impressed at all. Clearly, these people thought that they deserved the money and they took advantage of an easy process until they found themselves deeply in debt. They tried to maintain a lifestyle that they clearly could not afford. Had they invested the money they were using to finance their lavishness, in a few years they would have been able genuinely afford to live this way. Although this kind of overspending mentality seems to be more and more popular, this is not the right way to live.

Barely getting by with the skin of your teeth will never make you wealthy, no matter what possessions you may have. You can have a nice house and diamonds, but they can only get you but so far. In time people will realize that they are simply facades for poor money management and gross denial. So when I speak about believing that you can, I want you to be fully aware that this does not mean that you should go out and fake it until you make it, as they say. The Millionaire Father doesn't fake it in life, as faking it is totally dishonest and does not serve his children well. Faking it doesn't show integrity. And in time the fakers will all be exposed!

Faking it doesn't show integrity. And in time the fakers will all be exposed!

There is a time to stretch to get what you need in life. I realize that. However, you really don't need to live a million dollar lifestyle on a minimum wage income. If anything this sort of mentality will actually hinder your ability to believe in yourself. This sense of competition never allows you to realize what is at your disposal right now. It only makes you feel angry and somewhat jaded because you feel that you're missing out on something. Believing in yourself has everything to do with your ability to create more from what you have right now. It's not about parading around all of the trappings that makes people think that you are wealthy.

True wealth is not measured in the accumulation of things but rather in your ability to live for months and possibly years from your investments. The Millionaire Father is all about breaking the mentality that so many people have of living from paycheck to paycheck. The Millionaire Father concept teaches you how to save your paychecks rather than spend them carelessly.

Good Debt, Bad Debt

For the sake of our illustration we will call our next characters Tim and Sarah. Tim and Sarah owned a manufacturing company. After all expenses had been satisfied, they each had a net taxable income of $750,000 per year. They had been at this earning level for more than ten years. So combined they had earned 1.5 million in total net income annually. In a literal sense, this means that they acquired 15 million dollars over that period of time. For most people, that equals a sizeable amount of money.

They asked me for some financial advice as they were having trouble maintaining their monthly bills. I learned that they owned a house worth about one million dollars (which is not very high for their income level). The total mortgages on the property equaled $950,000 and other credit debts totaled about $6.3 million dollars. A debt of $6.3 million dollars is one that most people cannot fathom and rightly so. Most people could not grasp even having $6.3 million dollars, let alone owing that much in debt.

The only feasible way I could see them getting out of the hole they had dug for themselves was to go bankrupt or create a proposal to pay back some of their creditors, so I advised them to go see a bankruptcy trustee to get professional advise and see what their options were. Imagine clearing $120,000 or more each month and still not being able to make your minimum credit card payments. The point here is that it doesn't matter how much you make. What matters are your beliefs about money; that will determine how much you keep and save. The most basic way to become financially free and have more at the end of the month than just enough to pay your bills is by increasing your net worth and decreasing unnecessary debts.

 *A necessary debt is a debt that helps you to earn money and increase your net worth.*

Please note that I said unnecessary debts, which means that there are debts that are necessary. How do I define necessary debts? A necessary debt is a debt that helps you to earn money and increase your net worth. Any debt that you can use as leverage, to minimize your liabilities is a good debt. For example, the debt incurred through purchasing income properties is actually a good debt because the profits can go directly toward a savings account, long-term investment, or as a debt reducer. So then, that debt becomes a good debt because it directly or indirectly helps you to increase your net worth or in other words your overall profitability.

In addition to that, the property itself becomes an appreciating asset, which over time will be worth far more than you originally paid for it, meaning that you are again increasing your net worth by owning an appreciating asset. On the other hand most credit card debt is usually bad debt, as the purchases on credit cards are usually spontaneous, emotional and have no real value other than to yourself. Automobiles, although one is typically needed, overall are not the best choice to invest your money into, since they do not yield an actual return. Unless you own a cab service, or a limousine company, cars don't make you money.

They take money away from you. You spend money on the car every time it goes to the shop for oil changes, brake jobs, struts and shocks, engine and transmission repairs, and so on. You must put money into the car in order to keep it going. Yet the car does not directly earn a profit. You say, "Yeah but I need a car to get to work." Well, unless you are into sales which requires you to drive to several different locations weekly, your car really isn't a necessity, at least with regards to your work schedule. In many places, not all, you can actually take public transportation. My point here is that you have options.

It is when you exercise those options that you actually begin to actualize wealth. Buy assets, not liabilities. This is the secret to wealth. Invest in increasing assets. It's really simple. Assets are things that increase your worth. Liabilities are things that take money away from you. Now I am not suggesting that you should not enjoy yourself in life. I am only saying that there is a time and season for everything. It's not wrong for you to own a liability. You just need to know that liabilities won't help you to become The Millionaire Father.

Knowing That You Can Do It

You must believe you can do it. One of the myths about investing in real estate from the book, *The Millionaire Real Estate Investor,* is "I just can't do it" and the truth is, you don't know what you can or can't do until you try. I am great proof of this. If you talked to some of my high school teachers, they would have a different story on where I would be ten years after graduation than where I actually ended up being. If you had asked me, I wouldn't have known either. I had one teacher who said, "I'll read about you in the paper someday." He wasn't speaking about good press, but rather in a negative way.

Every time an article was written about me, I'd cut it out and mail it to him. His image of me had to change, because I believed in myself even when others chose not to. I always had the mindset that if someone else could do it so could I. Why would any other person be more capable than me? The truth was that nothing made me different at all from the next person. I may have had to work a little harder to get there. Rid yourself of false humility. The false humility crowd says, "I am happy with what I have." You are only repeating a self-defeating cycle handed down by your parents.

Okay, you may be satisfied with what you have but that doesn't mean that you shouldn't or can't strive for more. There will always be more, so why not take it? You MUST obtain financial wealth, that may seem a little strong, but it is and here is why I feel this way. Do you have any idea what you will need money for 5–25 years from now? What if your parent or spouse requires a special long-term care facility where the cost is $5,000 or even $20,000 a month to insure the best care? Are you currently in a situation to provide for your parents, or would the high health care cost far more than you could afford?

Perhaps, your child desires and deserves to go to college, yet you don't have the $50,000 per year to pay for the bill. Should money, or the lack of it dictate your child's education and ultimately his or her destiny? You really have no idea what you might need or even desire money for in the future. One thing is for sure; you will need money, and plenty of it for something. You owe it to yourself and your family to make sure the money is there when needed. Some will say it is selfish to desire wealth. I say it's selfish not to desire wealth.

 *Struggling financially or being wealthy are both planned. The good news: You get to pick.*

Your financial status right now is directly connected to what you believe. And what you believe is connected to the amount of information you have concerning a particular subject. If you have limited information about wealth, then you will only believe shallow thoughts concerning the possibility of your financial well-being. It is my hope that as you continue to read forward that your beliefs will be challenged to the core. In all fairness money doesn't actually grow on trees in the most literal sense. But one thing is for sure; money does grow. How does money grow? Well that's a process. The process begins with a complete rearrangement of thoughts, then a reordering of your habits.

Struggling from day to day and paycheck to paycheck is not accidental. Being wealthy is not accidental. They are both planned. I believe that as you begin to employ some of the many money tools that I will introduce to you, you will be on the road to recovery. Here is my honest disclosure to you, it won't happen for you overnight. No one gets into indebtedness overnight. It takes time. In the same manner, it will take time to get out of debt. However, having me as you personal mentor in this process, I can promise you that your distance from where you are to where you want to be will be shortened.

CHAPTER SUMMARY

- It is important that you believe you can do it, you are worth it and you deserve it.

- Having lots of money doesn't change you. It reveals who you really are.

- Everybody is investing in something.

- Wealthy people don't often look the part, and vice versa. Don't judge based on looks!

- We were put on this earth to do more than simply survive.

- There is such a thing as good debt.

- "I'm happy with what I have," is a self-defeating cycle handed down by your parents.

- You MUST obtain financial wealth—The future is uncertain.

3

NEVER SAY... MONEY ISN'T IMPORTANT!

Quite honestly, I make no claims about being a teacher of spiritual matters. I'll leave that job up to the spiritual masters of our day. But if there is one thing that I do know for sure, and have proven it over and again, it is this: the words that come out of your mouth matter far more than you would ever believe. Really, what you say actually has the ability to shape and re-shape your world and your experiences. Now if you ask me how this actually happens, I couldn't tell you. All I know is that it really works.

If you jump from a 30-story building what do you suppose would happen to you? Great, you know the answer, you'd prob-ably die. But unless you are Sir Isaac Newton or Galileo Galilei you probably don't know exactly how gravity works but yet you still respect its power. The same idea exists with the power of what you actually say. If you say I can't afford this house, then guess what, you won't be able to afford it. On the other hand if you say, I'm going to do whatever it takes to get into that house, then somehow it's going to happen for you.

Being a real estate specialist, I hear all kinds of things from various clients. Even though I am there with the primary pur-pose of being able to sell my clients a piece of property, I sure wish at times that I could digress for a moment and just deal with their words. Just dealing with what you say, will have a drastic affect on your total life, especially in the area of your finances. Far too often people tend to sabotage their own success by simply dooming themselves with their negative words.

Have you ever heard someone say that money isn't important? What a ridiculous statement; of course money is important! Money is essential to everyone's physical survival and emotional and spiritual well-being. Money bestows the means to provide for your family, the people that you love more than anyone else. Money also affords you the opportunity to help people who are in need all over world. Money can provide millions of people with food, clothing, clean water, and shelter. There is actually a scripture in the Bible that gives a clear description of how important money really is.

...money is the answer for everything. —*(Ecclesiastics 10:19 NIV)*

Money can actually make someone's last days on earth a heavenly blessing. It can also enhance the quality of your life during your entire stay here. Like I said before, many of us have been brought up to believe that money is something to be viewed in a negative way. It is often associated with negative morals and personality traits, such as greed and selfishness. We are conditioned from a very young age not to have any money or to get rid of it once it accumulates past the amount that common folks would approve of.

Perhaps you may feel as if your view on money and the words that you speak negatively about money are your parent's fault. No need to get mad at your parents, they were just repeating what their parents told them. Habits and traditions are usually passed down from one generation to the next. The good thing is that you now have the power to end this self-defeating cycle and teach your children about the good that money can do for them.

Money—An Intuitive Desire

Despite what you have heard about money, whether from your parents or friends, money is an inborn desire for most people. Do you remember looking through the couch cushions for change at a young age? Why were you searching so hard? You knew that money could do something for you. Even before you could truly understand the power of money, as a child you knew that it was necessary in order to buy you the toys and treats that you so desperately wanted. Having a few pennies in your possession meant that you had money; and you were beginning to feel important in the world.

 *It's what money does for a person that makes them feel empowered and liberated.*

So the point is this, before you actually were aware of your parents' opinion about money, you had already begun to form your own opinion. For the most part your opinion was pretty good, knowing the value of money and what it could actually do for you. Okay then, why is it that people desire money? Is it that money in and of itself has phenomenal value? Actually money is paper with dead people printed on them. If you take a match to money, it will be destroyed in seconds. So it's not that money has any real value.

It's what money does for a person that makes them feel empowered and liberated. And that is going to be different for everybody. For some, money gives them a feeling of worth and importance. Some guys like to flash their money around so that other people can look at them as a big shot. The truth is that money is really only important for what it can bring into your life. Money can buy us what so many of us want more of—time. The more money that you have accumulated, the less time you will have to dedicate to working hard long hours.

Money can create lasting memories with your family and loved ones. Whatever it is that is important to you, money can help you acquire that thing. I imagine based on that alone money then becomes an intuitive desire of ours. So that which you desire you cannot speak ill of otherwise it will leave you. Everybody has desire, and whatever your desire is, for the most part, money can help you to connect with that desire far more quickly and efficiently than any other means. Perhaps my greatest desire is being able to spend quality time with my family.

The truth is that money is really only important for what it can bring into your life.

I love my two boys more than anything in this world. And being able to watch them grow, learn, and enjoy this process called life is absolutely amazing. I wouldn't exchange it for anything in the world. Let's face it though, there are so few men who can actually say that they spend quality time with their children. It's not because they don't want to. Usually it's because they don't have enough time because they are working so tirelessly to try to meet all of the expenses and keep things moving.

Don't take that as a negative thing. I too would do whatever it takes in order to take care of my family, even if that meant working long tireless hours. I'm simply trying to convey to you that, you have options. You really don't have to work that hard, if you implement just a few of the strategies in the book that have worked for me over the years. But first understand that your desire is an inborn desire, and in some ways the desire for money can be seen as a twin to your desire since money usually has the ability to see your desire come true.

If my desire is to spend more quality time with my children then increasing my income will help me to do just that as I won't have to worry about how I am going to take care of this or that. Having enough money will afford me the privilege of focusing on the things I love most. Knowing this, I must commit to speaking words that affirm money and also affirm money working and flowing in my life. If I believe that money is supposed to be in my life, then I am going to speak it forth as if it is a natural "inborn" reality.

Focusing on the Benefits

Just for a minute think about what would you do if you didn't have to go work today? Possibly you might spend the entire day with your family and really get to know your children. There may be things about their personalities that you've never even had the time to notice before. If you don't have a family yet, maybe you would dedicate time to a local shelter and help people far less fortunate than you. If you never had to go to work, the possibilities would be endless in terms of what you could do with your free time. Financial wealth is the ability to live your life's dream and finance your vision without having to go to work every day. That of course is a huge benefit of having money.

Some people think that having a job that you are dedicated to promotes self-value and a good work ethic, especially with the hope that these two virtues may spill over into all aspects of your life. However, it is possible to value yourself and maintain a good work ethic without having to slave away at a mediocre job day after day. Your self-value should be inherently connected to your personality and it can be exemplified through having wealth. I always say, "The more good you can do for others, the more you should value yourself and others will value you." Seeing wealth from this perspective, how can having money be viewed negatively? How can anyone say anything other than good things about money?

 *In order to focus on the benefits you have to control what you hear and what you say.*

In order to focus on the benefits you have to control what you hear and what you say. What you say is always connected with what you've heard, so you may be able to save time and wasted energy fighting to get ahead financially by simply quarantining what goes into your ears. Have you ever heard someone say, "It is selfish to want wealth?" Most people don't have wealth. Far fewer understand wealth and how wealth actually works. Because of this we form prejudices about money. Isn't this how all prejudices form? Basically you judge a person, a place, an entire culture not based on what you know about them, but rather what you don't know.

When you do this you set yourself up for financial failure. Don't judge what you don't know about money. Instead learn whatever it is that you don't know about money and begin to educate your way to riches. When you begin to change the way you falsely judged money, you will change your focus and your words concerning money, and inevitably your money will change. It has to! Change your focus and you will change your outcome.

Let's try and look at wealth in a different way and use different words. Say, "It is selfish not to want wealth." If all kinds of good for others and yourself can come from your own personal wealth and you have the ability to make positive things happen, how selfish is it to not pursue wealth? What would the world be like if we had more millionaires doing more good to collectively help humanity? The world would be entirely different. While they are not the only examples of humanitarian efforts, just think about the contributions of Oprah Winfrey, Bill Gates, Warren Buffet, and rock star Bono.

 *When your money has a job to fulfill, then you will have an entirely new focus, which as I have said will yield you an entirely different return.*

Their contributions have not only affected the United States of America, where they all live, but also the continent of Africa. Their focus is entirely different. They believe that wealth is mandatory. Wealth only becomes mandatory when you have an actual assignment for your wealth to perform. Does your money have a mission? Or is your money just something that doesn't have a job to do? When your money has a job to fulfill, then you will have an entirely new focus, which as I have said will yield you an entirely different return.

If focusing on the benefits gets you what you truly desire let's list the many benefits that having more money will afford you. When you visually see what money can bring to you, then you will begin to say the right things about money, and money will begin to treat you the same way you treat it, with great respect! Don't just read this part, I need you to say it out loud, so you can hear yourself saying new powerful and positive words about money.

Money Affirmations for the Millionaire Father

- Money gives my children the best education available.
- Money allows me to take time off from work and travel the world, experiencing the vastness of other cultures.
- Money allows me to take great care of my family, feeding them well, sheltering them, and clothing them with the finest that life has to offer.
- Money helps me to help others in need. I can feed the hungry, help to pay medical expenses for those who cannot afford it, and provide shelter for the homeless.
- Money gives me the opportunity to help others experience their dreams.
- Money helps me to educate others who cannot afford the high cost of education.
- Money helps me experience my dreams.
- Money allows me the high honor of being able to care for my parents in their old age.

Of course this list could go one forever. However, this is a great start! It is when you begin to practice new ways of speaking about money that you create an environment that is conducive for the flow of money in your life. You may ask, why all this lesson about how to think about money and what to say about money? There is absolutely no need at all to talk about the practical side of money, if you don't really believe that you should have it. It'd be a waste of time to go into the details about real estate investing, financial planning and so on, if you didn't believe that money was for you. And the way that I can determine what you think about anything is by how you speak of it.

 *I have come to the conclusion that life is easier with money, PERIOD!*

If I asked you what you thought about your mother, hopefully you would begin to say some of the most remarkable things about her. If you began to speak ill about her, I would know right off that you had a pretty bad relationship. That being the case, I would also know that there is a very limited exchange between you and her. The same concept applies with money; the more freely you are able to talk about it the greater the relationship. Yes, money is a very personal thing.

Find Money Minded Friends

I have come to the conclusion that life is easier with money, PERIOD! My experience is that the people who say that money doesn't make life easier, typically don't have any money to begin with, so of course they view money negatively. If something is absent from your life, you cannot understand the positive aspects of that idea or thing. Their opinion really doesn't matter, and is usually based on wrong information. To them, money may mean a whole lot of bills, unnecessary worries, and a never ending cycle of working like a dog, producing feelings of desperation, depression and stress.

My father recalls that I made this statement when I was 20-years-old: "I will go to Disney World when I can afford to go and bring another family that isn't able to afford it." Even back then, I had big plans for my money. I committed myself to increase my ability. Well, in February 2009 this happened! I took a wonderful family of four to Disney World for seven nights. That was one the most incredible experiences I have ever had! Although I can't immediately end world hunger with my money, it doesn't mean that the small things I can do won't affect the world either.

One mystic says, "Look at your friends for your friends are a picture of what you are becoming."

Had I surrounded myself around people who did not think I could actually bring both my family and another to Disney, I would have never pulled it off. So you have to surround yourself with money minded friends, those who think the same kind of high thoughts that you think about money's ability to bring a new life to you. One mystic says, "Look at your friends for your friends are a picture of what you are becoming." I am very selective about my friends and whom I choose to hang out with. It's not because I'm some kind of big shot or anything, I simply understand the basics of how thoughts and words are transferred in life.

I've got some incredible plans in life, some of which I'll share with you in this book, others are much too big to share right now. However, it is my responsibility to make sure that I connect with people who will help to water the garden of my thoughts and ideas, not destroy it. So my friends are not those who are necessarily mutli-millionaires, but those who have the desire and capacity to become more than what they are right now. I surround myself with people who desire more out of life. When I connect with people who believe I can, it prevents me from dealing with the unnecessary struggle of having to fight through the negative opinions of people who fail to reach higher. Guard your thoughts, watch your words, and carefully choose your friends!

CHAPTER SUMMARY

- What you say matters!

- Money is essential to physical survival as well as emotional and spiritual well-being.

- You can trade money for time.

- Create money affirmations.

- Find money-minded friends.

4

SETTING GOALS

Setting goals is the first step in turning the invisible into the visible. —Tony Robbins

You may be reading this book thinking, "Wow, that Jeff Reitzel is a pretty smart guy. There is *no* way I can do what he does!" Well, let me tell you that I am a pretty average guy with no special training, upbringing or education. I didn't come from an exceptionally established or wealthy family and didn't have any special opportunities or treatment given to me along the way. If you ask my wife, I'm just a normal man trying to make a living and support my family, the people I cherish the most.

If there was something extra-special about me, then people could use that as an excuse for why they aren't achieving the kind of success they desire in life. They'd say, "Reitzel's had everything given to him on a silver platter in life." That just isn't true. Like most people, I had to work for everything that I've got. Along the way I just learned how to make better choices, and over time, I began to see the fruits of my labor. If there is anything that actually sets me apart from others, it is my desire to succeed and the fact that I take ACTION.

You can have as many goals, dreams and aspirations as the next person, but if you simply wait for them to come to you and don't do anything about getting them, they will never happen and you'll end up like everyone else, complaining about why life didn't work out the way it should have. So many people falsely believe that if they just have the desire in their minds, especially if it is a strong desire that they don't actually have to work for it. Truth is, you have to work hard and consistently to see your desires become a reality.

 *If you don't have desire then there isn't much of a starting point for you.*

Over the years I have helped so many people achieve their dreams and embrace their desires in life. There is one thing though that I have never been able to do, and that is to give someone desire. I know my limits and that's one of them. If you don't have desire then there isn't much of a starting point for you. Desire is the place where all of your dreams are launched. It is the place where you begin to build your goals upon. These goals can be in any area of your life—business, family, personal relationships, self-improvement, your spirituality, or even in the area of better health.

When you have desires in life you always have something to work towards. It is your desires that you create your goals around. For the most part, your desires can be easily connected to the thing in life that you enjoy doing. Usually the thing that you enjoy comes easy to you. It is when you set goals around that thing that you will begin to see wealth spring up.

What Do You Want In Life?

If I had to condense goal setting down to one concept or idea, it would all have to do with you and your desires. Your goals in life are going to be centered on what you want from life, nothing else. It doesn't matter what anyone else thinks or believes you should have. What matters most is what you really believe and what you truly have to have in life. The problem is that many people really have no clue exactly what they want out of life. They don't know where they want to go, what they want to do, what they'd like to see, or what they really want to accomplish.

This "lack of knowing" is not only unfulfilling, but is also one of the key reasons why people go to great lengths to fit into everyone else's world. Not being sure about what you want in life is a formula for disaster as people around you may use this to their advantage. What you are unsure about, other people will often try to fill that void in your life. Trust me when I tell you that you really don't need to have people filling those empty places within you. Don't get me wrong, I'm not suggesting that you don't receive advice or get counsel in life. You'll always need the expertise of knowledgeable people.

You must know what you want to achieve in life in order to touch your dreams.

What I am trying to convey is that you need to know what direction you would like to go in life so that you can start traveling in that direction. And that comes from within. You must know what you want to achieve in life in order to touch your dreams. Knowing what you want is the first step on your journey toward fulfillment. There are so many people who take far longer than necessary to get to where they need to go in life. Knowing what you want shortens your distance and helps you to avoid repeating self-defeating cycles.

So first you must get clear on what it is that you want. Don't be afraid to think outside of the box. You are in no way obligated to want what I want. But whatever that thing is, get clarity. If I want to travel to Toronto, I would have to know for sure that Toronto was really where I wanted to go. If all my friends were headed toward Montreal, I shouldn't follow them out of a sense of obligation. My goal is Toronto and going toward Montreal would put me on a totally different path to somewhere I may not belong.

Goals should be Specific

Let's get specific! What do you want to do? Where do you want to go? What do you have to have in life? Who do you truly desire to help? Getting clear on the answer to these kinds of questions can help you to become more specific about your goals. You will never reach a goal in life that you aren't clear about. In fact, your goals should be so clear that others could read it and easily put it into action. Goals should be transferable. It could be something simple like being able to spend more time with your family. Maybe you want to start your own business.

 *You will never reach a goal in life that you aren't clear about.*

Have you ever thought about sending underprivileged kids to college, helping to end genocide in Sudan, feeding the hungry, or even buying groceries for an elderly person on a fixed income? These are just a few primers that may help you to begin to think of some things that you can set as goals. Your specificity is actually what gets you moving, it's what causes action. Vague goals literally immobilize your dream and paralyze your vision. Okay, you're wondering what a vague goal looks like? Here are some vague goals; goals that are so unspecific that they do not create action.

Vague Goals:

I want to help people

I'd like to get involved

I wish I had more money

I need a better job

It'd be cool to have more time with my family

I'd love to travel places

I want to get more education

Those are all examples of vague goals because they do not have a specific point that will cause you to take real action. I call these goals more hoping thoughts, not goals. Goals are typically so concrete that they don't have much room for straying off the path. For example, a person may say I want to help people. What does that actually mean? What kind of people do you want to help? Where do they live? How do you want to help them? These are just a few qualifying questions that'll help you to get clarity on your goal. Again, it's your clarity that will enable you to reach your goals in life. Now let's look at this list of goals, a bit more refined, and consider what a difference clarity makes.

Specific Goals:

> I want to help feed hungry children in Guinea Bissau, Africa.

> I'd like to get involved in building affordable housing for seniors in Kitchener/Waterloo.

> I would like to increase my present income this year by $25,000 or more.

> I am looking for a job that will pay me a better hourly wage where all of my skills can be fully utilized.

> Every Saturday I plan on taking my family on an outdoor adventure.

> I am going to travel to Barcelona, Spain for my next vacation.

> I have chosen to enroll in a finance class at the University of Waterloo.

Can you see a difference in the language? The first list was rather vague, using open-ended language. The second list clarified the goal. All goals should be specific. The more specific you are in terms of where you would like to be financially in a year, or five years, the closer you will be to achieving that reality. Write your goals down. For example, you could write in 5 years I plan to earn $200,000 per year, and invest half of my income. That is much stronger than saying, "In 5 years I want more money." Simply saying it won't get you there; you've got to make it clear.

Write Down Your Goals

Writing your goals down as opposed to just saying them is always a good way to get started. Once you write something down, it repeats what you have already thought and literally embeds it in your memory. Children in school are taught to take notes so that the information they need to know for their test will be rehearsed in their memory since they wrote it down. I suggest that after you've written down your clear goals, that you put it somewhere that you can visibly see it as a constant reminder of where you are headed. You will be amazed at how effective this simple practice can be in motivating you to work towards what you really want in life.

 *Real Goal Setting has been one of the big factors contributing to my success.*

Real Goal Setting has been one of the big factors contributing to my success. This practice has also worked for many others. Not only is it important to have goals, but it is also important that these goals be relatively realistic to where you are in life at the time. It is not being realistic to say that you want to be a millionaire within three months time without having a phenomenal plan in place, or unless you hit the lottery. Such goals aren't realistic. If you make your goals too difficult to obtain, you may become discouraged and give up all together, putting you back at square one. So you must create goals for yourself that are achievable.

When I first started setting written financial goals, I was about thirteen. Most 13-year-olds I knew at the time just wanted enough money to buy movie tickets, food or clothes. I didn't focus on their smaller goals. I had much bigger plans. Someday, I felt that I would have so much wealth that I could do whatever I wanted in life. Did I know for sure what those things would be? Of course not, I was only thirteen; there was no possible way that I would be able to tell where I'd be in twenty years.

However, at the time, I still felt that it was important to get some goals written down on paper for myself. The simple act of just writing it my goals down on paper gave me a warm sense of accomplishment.

My first and most important goal was to be a millionaire by the age of 40. Back then I didn't know any millionaires personally, so I didn't really have anyone to mentor me in the process. So I had no clue how I was going to arrive at that point. All I knew was that I was determined to find a way. My writing it down was like writing a contract to myself, one that I refused to break. One of the things that you should understand is that when you write your goals down, and revisit them in your mind, your mind has the ability to find a way.

My writing it down was like writing a contract to myself, one that I refused to break.

The point here is that you really shouldn't worry about how it's going to happen. Just know that you really want it to happen for you and write your contract to yourself. My second goal was to be financially free by 45, meaning that I could pull in the same yearly income, even though I wasn't working. There again, I wasn't completely sure how this was going to happen either. All I knew was that it was possible, and that there were others that was able to do this, so why couldn't it happen for me?

Thirdly, I knew that in order for these first two things to happen, I would have to make at least $50,000 a year in income. This may not sound like a lot, but at thirteen I was already making $3,000 a year delivering papers. I would start off by writing a long-term goal down and then a roadmap on how I thought I was going to get there.

If I was 13 and wanted one million dollars by the time I was 40, I'd have to figure out what I would need to save per year, per month, on a weekly and even daily in order to reach that goal? If I wanted to make $50,000 per year what type of job would I need to have? What type of schooling would be required for this career? Of course, I was hoping that I wouldn't have to do any schooling, but I knew that a million dollars never comes without some kind of training.

Let's look at the goal of one million dollars in savings by the age of 40. At the time, I broke that down to $5,000 a year or $14 a day at a rate of return of 12%. That seemed like a lot of money per year but when I broke it down to a daily goal, I thought, surely I could save $14 a day. So now my massive goal of one million dollars was only $14 per day, an amount I'm sure most of us could spare to put away without enormous effort.

 *Little by little, not overnight, I saw each of my written goals becoming a reality.*

This is how I began to experience the life that I live today. Little by little, not overnight, I saw each of my written goals becoming a reality. As I got older, my goals changed from desiring financial wealth to wanting more time to dedicate to my family and just having recreational time. The burning desire that had previously motivated me to go out and make as much money as possible in the financial arena slowly faded, leaving me with the desire to be with my family as much as possible. Before, I only wanted a certain number of weeks off per year so I could go on vacation and relax.

Then, the number of hours I worked per week seemed like too many. Finally, as soon as I felt comfortable with my financial situation, I lessened the number of days during the week that I worked. Your goals may change from time to time, that's all right. Set big goals at the start, even bigger than you think you might be able to obtain. Let's look at the goal of reaching $50,000 in one year. I set this goal at age 13 because at that time, that seemed like a huge amount of money to me.

Today I look back and wondered why I thought so small. If you set a goal of reaching $100,000 income within 3 years, I can almost promise you that you will not go above that number as you have set that "limit" on yourself. What if you set your goal at $200,000 and you only reach $170,000? Does that mean that you failed? Keep in mind $100,000 is truly where you wanted to be and you hit $170,000. So shoot way beyond the skies and you may just fall upon a star.

The Benefit of Failure

Most people do not typically view failure as being beneficial. But failure can actually benefit you, especially when you use failure as a launching pad to improve and do greater things on the next go round. In essence when you have done all that you can do, you haven't failed even if you didn't reach your goal. You are now closer to your goal than you were before you started, and you have far more knowledge than you did as well. The only permanent failure is in not trying at all. So then failing to reach your goal should not be viewed negatively.

View it as a stepping-stone. Or you can look at what some people call failure as necessary education for the path you have chosen. I made a decision many years ago that cost me hundreds of thousands of dollars invested in bad stocks. Did I score big in the market? No, not at all. I lost miserably. However, looking back in retrospect I can now clearly see how I could have did things differently. Even in choosing my financial planner, I could have been far more diligent to check out his credentials and his track record at making money, not just for others, but for himself.

I could have been more sensitive to timing. I could have even educated myself more about the market so that I would have a working understanding of how the market worked. Had I done that I would have been able to not only appreciate expert advise, but also I would have been able to discern if someone wasn't what they claimed to be. So now I really don't see that as failure, but as a lesson learned. So in fact, that failure has helped me to reach my goal. Failures are not the end, but much more like a navigation system that immediately begins to reroute you once you've gone off track.

CHAPTER SUMMARY

- Desire is the starting point—you must know what you want to achieve in life in order to touch your dreams.

- Be realistic but set your goals higher than you think you can obtain.

- Goals should be specific—write your goals down.

5

UNDERSTANDING NET WORTH
AND PASSIVE INCOME

We just got through talking about goals and goal setting. Before you can reach your goals, you need to know where you are before you can get to where you want to go. You can't move onto the next grade in school unless your report card shows that you have done well enough in your classes to give you the privilege to move onto a higher grade, otherwise you'll have to repeat the grade until you get it right. The subject of net worth is a subject that unfortunately most people have not mastered. Most people do not know what their net worth is or why it is even important.

When I am out speaking to groups on investing I will often ask this question, "By a show of hands how many people in the room can tell me what their net worth is give or take $100.00?" For every 100 people in the room less than 5 people would raise their hands. That's less than 5 percent. That's a pretty crucial concern because it's often what you don't know in life that can hurt you the most. Your net worth statement is your financial report card.

One of the main reasons why people do not know how to improve their financial problems is because they don't really recognize that they have problems to begin with. If you do not know your net worth you are destined for nowhere good. So lets look at what net worth is. Your net worth is what you are worth financially. This has nothing to do with your intrinsic value. You may be the greatest, friendliest, and kindest person on earth. Those virtues are great. However, none of those things reflect positively on your personal financial statement.

So how does one determine your net worth, or what you are worth financially? Taking all of your total assets and subtracting your liabilities determine your net worth. The number that you get when you do this is your net worth. For some this number is very high, for many others this number may be in the negative, which is not good at all. But worse than being in the negative is not knowing where you are at all. For many years now I've made it a practice to look at my net worth statement daily. Some people say that this is a bit extreme, but this has worked very well for me. Besides that, it only takes me about 20 seconds.

My personal suggestion is that you take a look at your net worth statement at least once a month. Remember that what you focus on grows. Your net worth statement is about education and transformation. If you start out at "X" amount of money at the beginning of the year, you should have increased by the end of the year, if you understand how to increase. If you have not, then you may have to ask yourself was it even worth going to work for the entire year, having nothing to show for it.

My heartfelt desire is for you to understand that you do not have to work just to get by, or to simply pay bills. That's not life at its fullest. That's drudgery and painful. I've provided you with some charts, to show you how to determine your net worth. Some charts are far more detailed. However, the more detailed ones are typically associated with a higher net worth. If you are just starting out, then this chart will work just fine.

ASSETS THINGS OF VALUE THAT YOU OWN	VALUE ENTER VALUE IN THIS COLUMN
Home What is the value of your home? Enter that amount here. Contact a trusted Realtor to give you a range of how much your house is worth. Although their estimates are not exact, they do provide a good relative range for what your house value is. Don't worry about what you owe on the mortgage. Just enter the value.	
Automobiles What is the approximate value of all the cars you own? You can go to www.edmunds.com to find out how much your car is worth. Don't worry about whether or not your car is paid off. Just enter the total value of all your autos.	
Other Vehicles Other vehicles that you are able to register— Maybe you own a recreational vehicle, a boat, or motorcycle. Enter the total value.	
Household Appliances and Furnishings Estimate the total value of all your appliances, furniture, televisions, DVD players, surround sound systems, home theaters and electrical items. Remember do not give the value at time of purchase, but rather how much you can sell them for today. Enter the value	
Computers, Copiers, and Business Equipment What is the value of all your computers, copy machines, printers, cameras and other business equipment. Enter the value. (Continued on next page.)	

ASSETS (continued) THINGS OF VALUE THAT YOU OWN	VALUE ENTER VALUE IN THIS COLUMN
Jewelry Enter all of your fine jewelry, gold, silver, platinum, diamonds, or other fine precious stones. Enter the value.	
Savings and Checking Accounts How much money do you have in your checking and savings accounts now? No wishful thinking here, it doesn't matter what you want to have. What do you actually have right now? Enter the amount.	
Stocks All of the stocks that you own enter the present value.	
Mutual Funds Enter the value of your mutual funds here.	
Whole Life Insurance Policy Enter the value of your insurance policy that you can actually draw cash from. This is different than a term life policy, which can only be cashed in after you are dead. What is the cash value of your policy now? Enter the value here.	
Retirement Accounts Add up the value of your IRA's, 401(K) plans, RRSP's and similar types. Enter the value.	
Antiques and Specialty Items Think of any old items that you know are valuable, collector's items, books, old recordings, paraphernalia from famous people. Enter the total value here.	

LIABILITIES THINGS THAT YOU OWE	DEBT ENTER DEBT IN THIS COLUMN
Mortgages What is the total amount you owe on all of your mortgages? Be sure to include first, second, and third mortgages. Also remember that open lines of credit against your home are also considered as mortgages against your home. You can easily call your bank and ask them for the amount you owe. They will readily give you this information. Enter the total.	
Car, Boat, Motorcycle Loans What is the total amount of your loans for all of your vehicles? Enter that total here.	
College Loans Enter the loan amount.	
Credit Card Debt List the total amount of all your debt associated with credit cards. VISA, MasterCard, American Express, Diners Club, Discover, and ALL depart-ment store credit cards.—Enter the amount.	
Other Loans of Any Kind Enter here.	
TOTAL AMOUNT IN ASSETS	
TOTAL AMOUNT IN LIABILITIES	
Subtract the amount of your liabilities from the amount you have in assets and this is your **NET WORTH.** Enter Here.	

— SAMPLE CHART —

ASSETS	$
House	200,000.00
Car	15,000.00
Retirement Savings	20,000.00
Savings	2,000.00
Stocks	10,000.00
Total Assets	247,000.00

LIABILITIES	$
Mortgage	150,000.00
Car Loan	13,000.00
Credit Cards	15,000.00
Student Loan	20,000.00
Total Liabilities	198,000.00

TOTAL ASSETS	247,000.00
TOTAL LIABILITIES	198,000.00
So your NET WORTH would be	+$49,000.00

Hopefully you've enjoyed this exercise. I want you to get accustomed to doing this practice regularly, like I said earlier at least once a month. By the way, what's your grade? Okay you don't know how to grade yourself. I'll teach you. If you finished with a positive number, then you are doing all right. If you ended up in the negative, then you are not doing so well financially. Negative equals a bad grade. Please don't worry about this. The very fact that you now know how to evaluate your net worth actually increases your grade because now you are aware. Awareness brings increase.

Increasing Your Net Worth

So there are ways of increasing your score, which means that you have a high positive number in the NET WORTH box. The first thing that you need to understand is that you must buy assets, but real assets, not just any kind of asset. If you go out and buy a whole lot of jewelry and a fleet of cars, unless you are selling cars and fine jewels, you've actually purchased something that you've immediately lost value on the moment you purchased it. Things that only have sentimental value to your and your family may not qualify as being actual assets.

Simply, an asset is something that makes you money.

Real simply, an asset is something that makes you money. So then, your house is probably the most obvious asset since you can make money by owning a home. Some real estate professionals tend to say that only investment property actually makes you money, not the house you live in. I totally disagree with this thinking. The house you live in makes you money whether you rent it out or not, since it is an answer to you not renting from someone. That's a savings right there. Instead of paying out rent money each month, your mortgage payment is going toward decreasing your principle and interest on your mortgage.

The house you live in makes you money whether you rent it out or not, since it is an answer to you not renting from someone.

That is making you money on the most basic sense. Of course investment property can have the ability to produce money-making results far more quickly. But real estate in general is an asset that has proven to increase over time. Even if your property goes down in value because of a bad market, it will resurge at some point in the future. Stocks are assets also, however they are a bit more speculative as they can go down, way down, to the bottom. You can lose big in the stock market as many of us have seen in the past decade.

At the same time, there are people who have made billions and billions of dollars through solely investing in the stock market. So stocks are assets. Cash is an asset. Have you ever heard the phrase, "Cash is King"?

Cash can make you money, so it qualifies as an asset. The car you drive can be an asset if the car helps you to get money. So my point here is to get you to at least become comfortable with knowing what an asset is, and then buying assets. Although I did not list it, a business is also an asset if it is profitable. So buying assets will quickly increase your net worth. Decreasing your liabilities will also increase your net worth.

A liability is anything that doesn't make you money, but rather takes money away from you. Get rid of loans, not all, but the ones that are not increasing your money. There are some debts that I actually encourage, because certain debts can make you money. For example getting a mortgage for an investment property is definitely a debt, yet that debt has proven many times to make many people rich.

This is one of the concepts that have brought riches into my life. Borrow other people's money to buy and manage assets, this is a sure way to wealth. The whole study of net worth can definitely become more complex especially as you climb the financial ladder, but for starters, remember assets make you money, and liabilities take your money. If you've learned that much, then we are ready to move forward.

Passive Income

Once you have fully understood net worth and why it is so important to know yours, there's one other thing that you should also know and that's passive income. Okay, you know how to grade yourself on your net worth. Well what's your score on your passive income? Like net worth, the subject of passive income is rarely taught in the home, and there are many business schools that never bring up the topic either. Well I'm here to tell you that your passive income can be even more important than your net worth. Let me explain.

Passive income is income that you don't have to go to work to create. Passive income happens even when you are relaxing. I call it money working for you instead of you working for money. A good example of passive income is rental property that requires little effort on your part to maintain. While real estate is one of the great examples of this, you can also get a passive income from investing in stocks, bonds, or receiving residual income from royalties and intellectual properties such as books and musical compositions.

Here is the key; until you have a passive income the same amount or greater than your current income you can't truly be financially free, that is why this is so important to discuss. Let's say you have an income of $50,000.00 and you just want to replace that over a period of time, you are going to need to have enough assets or businesses that produce that income. What if you only wanted to invest in bonds and the bonds you purchased could yield you a return of 5% per year ($50,000.00/.05= 1,000,000.00) this means in order to have an income of $50,000.00 per year from bonds returning 5% you must have $1 million invested in bonds.

Here is the key; until you have a passive income the same amount or greater than your current income you can't truly be financially free

I'm not recommending that bonds or any other investments in particular is where you should invest. I'm simply illustrating how to figure out if you are on the right track for where you want to be financially. Let's say you are 50 years old and have $900,000.00 currently invested in bonds and want to be financially free by the time you are 55, then you are likely on the right track. On the flip side if you are 50 years old and currently have $100,000.00 invested in bonds more than likely you are going to either need to change your time frame or find another investment vehicle or maybe a combination of both.

At that rate of return and for the time that you want to invest, getting that kind of yield is not going to happen. So then you will have to find the kind of investment that will be most suitable for your needs. Remember, everybody is different and you ought to find the investment that you are most comfortable with. More than that, you've got to find the investment that works best for you.

We will talk more about different investments in the next chapter. Just remember this: before looking at different investment options you need to know—

1) What you are investing in.

2) Whether or not the investment will get you the results that you are looking for in the time period that you need them to.

If what you are actually investing in is going to get you where you desire to be, then congratulations! You are doing well and should continue on the same path. Don't worry about what anyone else says. Typically when people are on the right track there are always distractions that will come up from time to time to get you off course. If what you are doing is working, if it's legal, and creating for you a passive income, keep on doing it.

On the other hand, if what you are doing isn't going to get you where you need to be, then be humble enough to get professional advice from a qualified financial consultant, who should be able to offer you some options that will work best for you. There are several vehicles that can get you where you want to go, my personal favorites are Residential Real Estate and Owning Businesses. We will talk more about both.

As a recap invest in what you understand or are willing to commit to learning about. From my years of experience when you don't know what you are investing in, you are bound to lose more money than you could imagine. So practice diligence, but don't be afraid to listen to your gut. That intuitive voice on the inside of you, that usually points you in the right path.

CHAPTER SUMMARY

- Net worth and passive income are your financial report cards.

- Until you have a passive income the same or greater than your current income you can't be truly financially free.

6

INVESTING—WHERE DO I BEGIN?

There are basically four things that you can do with your money. You can spend your money. This is the one area that I don't really have to teach people how to do. Most people know all too well how to spend their money, which is why they have so little of it. Perhaps I will write a book dedicated to proper spending habits, the "how-tos" of spending. Spending is fundamentally giving someone your money in exchange for something that you perceive is of equal or fair value. For now, just know that spending is one of the four things you can do with your money.

You can save your money. This is simply setting your money aside for a designated purpose or for future need. Saving is obviously more difficult than spending because it takes discipline to save your money. Investing, which we shall talk about takes financial literacy to do. But if you have a hard time saving your money, you'll probably have an even harder time investing it. Each level in this ladder requires more knowledge, skill, and at times spirituality. The last thing that you can do with your money, which is perhaps the highest level of stewardship, is to give it away.

You can also lend your money. Lending is either profitable or unprofitable. If you lend your money with interest as the banks do, then you will be highly profitable. If you lend your money without interest, or to someone who has a track record of not paying back, then you may have made a poor decision in lending your money. Lending is one of the things that you can do with your money, and can be a great way to increase your net worth, if you do it correctly.

Give
Invest
Lend
Save
Spend

Giving is by far the highest level of money management, especially when you give to merit worthy causes. Giving shows that you are mature in the process of money management and that you freely exercise a grateful attitude for everything that you have. But just before we reach the top of this pyramid lets look at investing. Investing is perhaps the most complex of the four to understand. Most people know how to spend. Few people exercise the discipline to save. With giving, you either give or you don't. It's that simple.

The Basics of Investing

With investing there are a few basics that you need to know. Investing is the one of the best ways to create wealth. This isn't the only way to create wealth, as we can see from entertainers, movie stars, and musical performers, and professional athletes. They create wealth through tapping into the reservoir of their own creative self. In many ways they too have invested in order to receive the great return through practice and long rehearsals. So if you want to be wealthy and you haven't been left a major inheritance, it's going to come through some type of investment.

 *The first thing that you must get settled on is the "why" of your investing.*

The first thing that you must get settled on is the "why" of your investing. Why are you investing? What is your sole objective? For each person this will be different. Many people invest for retirement so when they reach their mature adult years they have something to draw from. No one should have to work forever. When the time comes that you no longer can work or desire to work, your investments should be able to take care of your needs as a replacement to your loss or reduced income. This is why many people invest. They invest for the golden years.

Most young people in their twenties don't think about retirement because for them that whole concept seems so distant. For some the thought doesn't even cross their mind because they feel as if they are going to live forever and ever. I can remember those days, and yes, that is a great feeling to have. But it's just not realistic. No matter how young you are, how healthy you are you are going to get older someday, and when you do you are going to need to draw from that which you have invested earlier on.

Another reason why people invest is to pay for large items that they will inevitably need in the future. For example, I have two of the most wonderful boys in the universe. At this stage they are being provided for well. They have everything they need. As they get older though their needs are going to change, and with those changes come expenses. College can be costly, and the average person doesn't have $40,000 disposable income sitting around each year times the amount of children that you have. I know that there are several colleges that are far less expensive, but for the most part college can be a hefty payment.

 *Investing can then be looked at as safeguard.*

There is always the alternative of getting a student loan, but it's really no fun starting your first day at work, fresh out of college, owing more money than you'll make your entire first year. If you can give your child a fresh start in life, then by all means do so. But in order to do that, it'll take some pretty intentionally investing strategy. So you can invest for you kids college tuitions. If you have daughters you may want to invest for those weddings that may come down the road. Even the house you live in, you may want to upgrade and purchase the home of your dreams.

The more elaborate the house the higher your down payment may be. So you are going to want to invest for your home.

As unfortunate as this may sound, some people may need to invest in the case that tragedy occurs to have something to lean back on. Divorce can occur, sudden death can occur, and also sickness that can be exorbitantly expensive can happen at anytime. When it does, then you will have to be ready to deal with the financial obligation that goes along with it. Investing can then be looked at as safeguard.

One of the things you may want to do is leave an inheritance for your children. If they are adults when you pass away and you have taught them right, they will best know what to do with the money. Be very careful when you start to attract wealth that you don't spoil your kids, its very possible that the more you give them the less they will have over time. I must thank my father from the bottom of my heart for never giving me money for anything, ever! (Ok I did receive a few dollars a week allowance as a kid)

The basics of investing begin with you knowing why you are investing. You are responsible to take action and make sure that your family has the best start in life. We don't blindly invest. We invest with a purpose in mind.

Investing For Someone Else

My father-in-law, Dave Denomme is a die-hard Detroit Red Wings fan and has been for more than 55 years. For whatever reasons he hadn't been to a Red Wings game in nearly 30 years but has religiously watched every game on TV. For the 2009 Stanley Cup Playoffs I decided to start taking him to games. Well that turned into going to every game of the playoffs, all the way to Game 7 of the Stanley Cup Finals, including driving to the games in Pittsburgh, Pennsylvania.

The joy and excitement on his face every day was like giving a 5-year-old their very first bike. My wife asked me once,

"Doesn't the eight hours of driving for each game get tiring?" I said, "The WHY is so great that I haven't ever thought about the driving." Each trip has been a joy and I have precious memories that will last a lifetime. On one of the trips back home to Canada from Detroit, I remember we started talking about cars. Dave told me that his dream car ever since he was a child was a black on black convertible Mustang, that was a Thursday night when he told me this.

Saturday morning he had a black on black convertible Mustang sitting in his driveway. You should have seen the look on his face. My kids shouldn't have heard the words he said, but of course he was overjoyed and really didn't know how to express himself with English words. The man was so happy, and I was so glad to enjoy the moment with him. That was the best purchase I ever made and it wasn't even for my personal benefit. At the time of this writing I am actually leaving tomorrow with my father in law, on our way to Sweden to see the Red Wings opening game for the 2009/2010 season.

Your money is best used when it can in turn help someone to enjoy life.

Maybe you are thinking that the gift was spending the money on hockey tickets. No not at all. The cost of the games wasn't the gift. The gift was being able to spend my time with him. You see money is Good for the Good that it can do! So in all actuality my father in law can enjoy his life at a higher level because of the investments that I made. It's not always about you, sometimes your investment will help you to help someone else.

Your money is best used when it can in turn help someone to enjoy life. So even if you are young, it still makes great sense to begin investing now. Even while you are still young, if you've properly invested you can help your parents, in laws, or whomever you so choose, because you invested with a cause. Again you must get clear on the cause in mind. So even if as a young person, you don't fully understand the value of investing for your future, you can invest for someone else's.

Different Kinds of Investments

Here I would like to introduce some of the more common kinds of investments that many people have heard of yet may not know how they actually work. This is only for information not recommendation. It is my firm belief that you should always go to the experts to get the advice you need. So you need to find a qualified financial planner to help you tailor make a plan that works best for you. There are hundreds of different types of investments. Allow me to introduce you to a few. I've dedicated an entire chapter to real estate investing so we will talk more about that in that chapter.

A stock—is a portion of the ownership of a corporation. A share in a corporation gives the owner of the stock a stake in the company and its profits. If a corporation has issued 100 stocks in total, then each stock represents a 1% ownership in the company. Stocks are also known as an equity or share.

A bond—is a debt security, whereas the authorized issuer owes the holders a debt and, depending on the terms of the bond, may pay interest (the coupon) and/or to repay the principal at a later date, which is called maturity. A bond is a formal contract to repay borrowed money with interest at fixed times. So in plain terms, a bond is like a loan: the *issuer* is the borrower (debtor), the *holder* is the lender (creditor), and the *coupon* is the interest

Bonds and stocks are both securities, but the major difference between them is that stockholders have an equity stake in the company. Stockholders are in essence owners of the company. Bondholders have a creditor stake in the company since they are the lenders. Bonds usually have a defined term, or maturity date, after which the bond is redeemed, whereas stocks may be outstanding for an indefinite period.

A mutual fund—An open-ended fund operated by an investment company which raises money from shareholders and invests in a group of assets. Mutual funds raise money by selling shares of the fund to the public, much like any other type of company can sell stock in itself to the public. Mutual funds then take the money they receive from the sale of their shares and use it to purchase various investment vehicles, such as stocks, bonds and money market instruments. This is why mutual funds are so diverse. In return for the money they give to the fund when purchasing shares, shareholders receive an equity position in the fund. For most mutual funds, shareholders are free to sell their shares at any time, although the price of a share in a mutual fund will fluctuate daily, depending upon the performance of the fund.

A CD—Certificates of Deposit (CDs) or commercial paper are considered to be money market instruments and not bonds. CDs are short or medium-term, interest-bearing, FDIC-insured debt instruments offered through your local bank or credit union. CDs offer higher rates of return than most comparable investments. CDs are low risk and low return investments. They are usually kept in an account anywhere from 3 months to six years.

How To Hire A Qualified Financial Planner

In order for you to know which of these investments are going to work best for you, you will need the advice of someone who is working with these investments regularly. If you wanted to get a house built, you wouldn't go to a baker, because he wouldn't have the expertise for building homes. You would go to someone who was qualified and had a proven track record because what you are asking him or her to do; they have already done for themselves successfully. I've gotten in quite a bind before with financial planners because I wasn't as forthright about asking for certain information as I am today.

Look for a financial planner that has made other people money.

When looking for a financial planner you want to know that your planner has a track record based on the fact that he or she has made other people money. So then, you need to ask him if he has referrals. Ask your family and friends if they already have a planner with whom they are satisfied. This doesn't necessarily mean that you won't be disappointed after getting referrals; it just reduces the likelihood of running into problems. You don't have to be ridiculous, asking for thousands of referrals, three or four will do. You just want to get a feel for how this person deals with money, other people's money, more importantly your money.

Here is the thing that I wish I had done in my first experience with a financial planner, ASK FOR THEIR PERSONAL FINANCIAL STATEMENT. I know that sounds a bit crazy, and possibly intrusive, but when you really think about it, it's not.

Why would you want to invest your money with someone who cannot handle their own money? That doesn't make any sense. Would you want to learn to fly from someone who hasn't flown a plane? Of course not! So why would you invest your money with someone who doesn't have financial integrity?

There are so many people today who are parading around as financial planners yet can hardly balance a checkbook. I'm not suggesting to you that the planner has to give you're their personal statements, they don't. However, any planner who willingly offers that information to you will make you feel more comfortable about dealing with them. Okay you ask, "What if they are just starting out, then what?" Great question! I don't have a problem with newcomers. In fact, I really like young aggressive go-getters. I love giving people a chance.

When I was very young, I started in the real estate business, and people trusted me. So I want to return the favor. I just would be careful not to give my entire portfolio to someone who is just starting out. What I would do is give him or her a small portion to work with and as they begin to produce, I will give them more and then some more. Using this method, I would have a much better feeling of comfort knowing that I will give more as I am able to trust them.

One mistake that I've made that I am instructing you to avoid is not to become overly trusting of a financial planner solely based on the fact that he or she has been in the business for a long time. Being in business a long time is not the determining factor that a person is qualified. Being in business and helping others to increase their net worth through your investment strategies is a great determining factor. My advice to you, is ask questions, not a million, just enough for you to feel comfortably sure that you are dealing with a financial planner who knows how to increase your financial portfolio.

CHAPTER SUMMARY

- Why are you investing? Figure this out first.

- Your money is best used when it can in turn help someone to enjoy life.

- Understand the different options before investing.

- Hire a qualified financial planner.

7

THE COMPANY THAT YOU KEEP

"The key is to keep company only with people who uplift you, whose presence calls forth your best."
—*Epictetus (Greek philosopher associated with the Stoics, AD 55-c.135)*

We've dealt with figures, charts and net worth calculations, now let's take a more personal course. One of the things that I have come to understand, and I am still becoming more aware of this with each day that I live, is that there is more to becoming The Millionaire Father than just facts and figures, and crunching numbers. It goes deeper into your personal character. Much of being a great dad is about the example that you live before your children. I'm a businessman, not a cleric, so I'm not preaching to you, just talking to you about real life stuff.

So many fathers fail to understand that in order to reach the levels that they are capable of reaching in life, they are going to have to make a decision to eliminate some uninspiring company. You are the company that you keep, and your friends are a clear indication of what you are or what you will become. So it is very important whom you have in your inner circle of company. I'm in no way trying to tell you that everyone who doesn't think like you are necessarily bad people. I'm merely saying be careful to choose the people whom you have in your inner circle.

The people who live in your inner circle need to be people that are supportive of where you are going in life. Since this work is about development and becoming the kind of father and provider that produces great children and families, you need to find people whose values support yours. One of the things that can be most counterproductive is when you are trying to become more fiscal minded yet you surround yourself with people who constantly think low thoughts especially as it relates to money. I am fortunate to work in an environment where for the most part, my staff and peers typically think win/win and on the up and up.

Most of the people that I associate myself with want to do more and have more in life. Since that is the case, I never have any problem or conflict with them with regards to my dreams and goals. Someone once said never share your 16 x 20 dream with people who only have 5 x 7 minds. You have to be very aware that there are dream stealers and dream killers out there waiting to suffocate your effectiveness and your goals before they become a reality. My advice is to stay clear away from them. Your family and your commitment to them should be at the very top of the list of things that you have to do in life.

Everything else is secondary. You have to ask yourself the question, "How does everything that I do line up with my goals?" Does your choice of who you associate with line up with your goals? Do your friends and close hanging partners believe in your dream? Do they have dreams themselves? Or do you often find yourself having to defend your dreams because they simply don't understand why you think so big? If you are in this situation you may have to reconsider who you consider to be your friends in life.

 *"How does everything that I do line up with my goals?"*

Real friends in life always do their best to support you in anything that you are doing that will move you in an upward direction. True friends don't try to pull you down. So what has worked for me is that I try my best to associate with people who think increase thoughts not decrease thoughts. Dealing with people who always talk about negative things will eventually weigh you down. So you have to reconsider who you choose to dwell in your inner circle from your outer circle to the one that needs to be totally outside the circle all together.

Everybody may have a place in your life, but you get to decide exactly where that place is. The ones closest to you are those that can help to give you counsel, helping you to stay on the path that you have chosen. In many countries the President or King or whomever is the head of that country often have an advisor. Their advisor's job is to give the President advice that supports them in executing their plan in the most beneficial way. The advisors job is not to usurp authority over the President or to create a private agenda.

Everybody may have a place in your life, but you get to decide exactly where that place is.

That is the same way that the company in your life should be. They are there to support your goal. My goal is to create such a storehouse of riches that I can supply all the good that my family desires and also help bring good to people who need help in various places. In order to do that, I am going to have to create many wealth opportunities. So I want people around me who can help me to do that quickly, efficiently, and most of all effectively.

The Advice of Others

One of the things that you have to do is get advice from people who are qualified to give you advice. I'm always a bit surprised when people who have never owned a house or any investment real estate offer such strong advice on the subject. It's kind of amazing when totally unqualified people try to tell you how to become successful when they have never succeeded at doing anything in life. Remember that advice is only as good as the source that it is coming from. Everybody has something to say in life. And that's fine!

Just be sure that what's being said, or shall I say what you are hearing is credible. When it comes to investing in anything from stocks and bonds to real estate, you'll always have a group of people who will try their best to talk you out of making the necessary move to secure property, open up a business, or to purchase a rising stock. They'll say things like, "I wouldn't invest right now if I were you." "It's not the best time to invest, you ought to wait ten years or more." It's talk like that that causes people to lose big in life.

If you are a winner, and I know that you are because you are reading this book, beware of what anyone has to say to try to steer you in any other direction than success. Get advice from the pros. If I wanted to buy a Cadillac I certainly wouldn't get advice about the car from someone whose never owned one, that wouldn't make sense at all. I'd find someone who has driven the car and ask them questions about their satisfaction and the overall customer service that they receive from the dealer.

If you want advice on how to make it in real estate, get it from a real estate investor, not your cousin Joey, unless of course, Joey is an investor. Hopefully you are getting my point. Who you surround yourself with will eventually become your reality. Since you are a winner connect with other winners and as Zig Ziglar says, "I'll see you at the top."

CHAPTER SUMMARY

- You are the company you keep—find people who share and support your values.

- Real friends always do their best to support you.

- Everyone may have a place in your life, but you get to decide exactly where that place is.

- Only take advice from qualified people.

8

LEVERAGE INVESTING

A term that has become rather popular within the past fif-teen years or so is leverage investing. The whole concept of leverage investing is that you leverage the equity in your home or other property and use the proceeds from that to finance investment real estate, new start businesses, or to invest in promising stocks. There are many people who have successfully used this method to become financially free in a short amount of time. The basic idea is that you borrow money in order to make more money by investing your money into a vehicle that can potentially create a positive cash flow for you.

Personally, I am a firm believer in the whole concept of leverage investing. It has helped so many people to get ahead in life. There are, however, possible pitfalls. The most obvious is that you can lose everything if you don't know what you are doing. You should really be properly advised with regards to this. The two things that I have seen that have caused problems in this area are greed and ignorance. Worse yet, is when both greed and ignorance are coupled together, that's surely a destructive force. Leverage investing is a good thing but even a good thing can turn bad if you began to abuse its original purpose.

My Story on Leverage Investing

Let me share with you my personal journey with investing and how it led me to the concept of leverage investing or what I call "borrowing to invest." Well, I was 14-years-young at the time, and had figured out that investing in general was a pretty good idea. So I started investing in mutual funds and stocks, as that was all I knew about at the time. When I was in high school I had a part time job at Wendy's, and during my first full year there I managed to save $800.00 per month. By the end of the year I had $10,000.

Leverage investing is a good thing but even a good thing can turn bad if you begin to abuse its original purpose.

A lot of people look at that and think, wow wasn't that a hard thing to do at such a young age? My answer would be no, it was very easy. At 14-years-old, I had no need for money whatsoever. I didn't have a driver's license, so there was no need to own a car. I'd been living with my parents since birth, so there was no need for rent or mortgage payments. My parents paid for all of my daily food and they clothed me. For me it was very easy to save. Beyond that, it takes time to spend, and if I wasn't at school I was at work.

By the end of the year my investments had grown to $11,000.00 and this really started to excite me. I received $1,000.00 for what I perceived as doing nothing. After seeing how well this worked, I then started mapping things out to see where this could potentially take me if I continued doing the same thing over a longer period of time. Using this basic style of investing, I calculated that I would have roughly $9.5 million dollars at age 55. Well this number blew me away, and still does today. Who would ever need $9.5 million dollars?

Then I got to thinking, 40 years seemed like a long time away and 55-years-old seemed really old. Remember I was only 14 at the time, so 25 seemed sort of old to me. I started reading more and learned about leverage investing and then got my calculator out and took a look at what a $130,000.00 loan would cost me per month. At the time it would have been $800.00 per month. So I thought $800.00, I can afford that, that's what I'm saving now anyway. So if I invested $130,000.00 if the market went up 10% the first year, I would have a gain of $13,000.00.

If I just invested $800.00 a month like I was doing my gain would only be $1,000.00 for the first year. Then at the start of my second year I would have a $143,000.00. Well at the end of the 40-year-period I would have approximately $13.5 million dollars. Wow, that's $4 million dollars for free! How did this work? The way this works is that you have a larger sum of money to start with, so the whole idea of compounding (compound interest) takes over. Ok now I had my plan, so my next move was to go to the bank to show them my wonderful plan and have them lend me $130,000.00.

How could they refuse this perfect plan? I had a proven track record of handing an $800.00 commitment. Well guess what? They said no, though not totally. They did agree to lend me $10,000.00 to start with. Then I proved myself for a period and they bumped it up to $25,000.00 then to $75,000.00 and eventually $155,000.00. That was my start in investing, and I've been investing ever since. I knew not to be careless and to investigate all of the facts. That is why I became successful at doing this. Not everybody is as cautious as they should be. With leverage you are using money you actually don't have so you have to use extra care and caution, as you have to be accountable for not only your money but the leveraged money as well.

Other Real Life Examples

Allow me to use some true-to-life examples to illustrate my point. Consider, Josie a 29-year-old single, aggressive go-getter, who works full time as a paralegal for one of Toronto's top law firms. Josie received a promotional invitation to attend a one-night informational session about leverage investing. In that three-hour session she heard tremendous strategies on how to borrow money for her down payment to purchase new properties. Josie also learned that the people who had really good credit were more likely to get approved for the loans than those who had marginal credit.

Josie, who had excellent credit decided from that one night seminar to try her luck at this new business concept. The very next day she began to search the newspapers and the internet searching for what she believed was great real estate deals in the her area. She found a multi-family building that she needed forty thousand dollars for her down payment. The building was $400,000. The house she owned was worth $185,000 and she owed about $125,000, which meant that she had $60,000 in equity.

She borrowed $40,000 for her down payment and quickly closed on the loan for her new multi-family real estate. What Josie failed to do was to investigate any details about the property she was buying or how good the actual deal was. The property that she purchased happened to be in the worst area of town. That isn't always the most significant problem; as some not-so-nice areas can still produce a positive cash flow if the tenants pay their rent. The taxes (percentage) on the property were twice the amount that she paid on her own home, which was in a quaint suburban town, three towns over.

This particular multi-family had four units, one of which had been vacant for seven months, the other more than a year. She failed to take the time to crunch the numbers to get an understanding to see how this property would actually yield her a positive cash flow. All she saw was the fact that she could actually get into another piece of property with very little effort. The fact that this property was in the shoddiest part of town would become more of a problem if she ever decided to sell the property, as properties in undesirable areas are not as marketable to the masses as properties in decent neighborhoods.

Again, I am not saying that you cannot make a significant profit from investments in undesirable neighborhoods; people do it all the time. In fact, I know people who earn a significant income from income properties in these areas. The people who are successful at making profit in these areas are people who are quite familiar with the area, the people, and the overall process. Unfortunately, Josie not only lost her income property within fourteen months but six months later the house she lived in was in pre-foreclosure. Her credit was marred as she was forced to file for bankruptcy to save what little she had.

Why did this happen? Josie went headlong into a very lucrative profession not knowing what she was doing. She was not trained to understand the up's and down's of the leverage investing. Because of her ignorance of the bigger picture of leverage investing, she lost more than she was comfortably able to lose. This story could have been totally different had she taken the time to fully investigate all the options.

Another option is that she could have contacted a qualified realtor who was well versed and understood leverage investing and the housing market. They would have been well able to coach her along in her process. Instead, with limited information she went out and tried to substitute her aggressiveness for smarts and common sense. In the end, she lost big-time.

Scott, who is a student by night working on his MBA, and an auditor by day at a large auditing firm, also sells real estate on the weekends. Scott, a hopeful Millionaire Father, married for three years, has two young children, a boy and a girl. Scott was able to squeeze in time to attend the same one night seminar that Josie attended. At the end of the seminar Scott chose to continue learning about leverage investing.

Being a part time realtor and having sold at least 20 homes in the past three years, Scott felt pretty knowledgeable about the subject of leverage investing. But being the student that he is, he always welcomed more knowledge on the subject. Having excellent credit like Josie, Scott knew that he could use the equity in his starter home to quickly increase his net worth and get him on the path to riches. After completing the premium level three-day course on leverage investing, Scott went out to work his newly learned skills in this vast market.

Scott borrowed money against his house, playing it really safe at first, and only getting properties that he could afford. The success was instant. He began to see a positive cash flow after his first purchase. This excited him so much; that he nearly became possessed with what he thought was the easiest way to make money on earth. Scott kept getting houses. By the end of the year, he was up to nine multi-family properties, having to carry mortgages on all of them. Scott's marriage became an increasing strain, as he was an absentee father and husband, spending no time with his family at all, trying to achieve super success in life.

Not fully factoring in the potential problems with regard to upkeep, Scott didn't foresee that he would have to fix the flat roof on his six family unit that would cost him $40,000 to properly repair. At the same time he lost four of his best paying tenants who were excited about purchasing their first homes for their families. In one of his properties the hot water heater burst, and the repair estimates came in between $13,500–$17,500. Fortunately, Scott had insurance that partially covered that unforeseen repair bill. With his copayment he would only have to pay $5000.00 of the bill, the insurance company would pay the remaining balance.

 *Like many people who become obsessed with greed, they overextend themselves...*

What caught Scott totally off guard was that he didn't have any savings in reserve to maintain the properties. Instead of putting money aside each month, Scott lavishly spent on himself, his wife and children, buying fancy things that he thought would substitute for spending quality time with his family. He became greedy and wound up biting off more than he could chew. Like many people who become obsessed with greed, they overextend themselves, and instead of pulling back, they just continue to do the same thing that got them in their situation.

What Scott should have done, was set aside a percentage of his rental income in an account designated for these types of required maintenance costs. Scott was not totally ignorant of how leverage investing worked, but refused to pay attention to some of the underlying details that could make or break him.

There are so many people who share the same stories as Josie and Scott.

The worst-case scenario would be Josie Scott, a combination of both ignorance and greed, a sure formula for failure. As it has always been my heart to help people get ahead financially in life, I needed to share these examples with you so that you don't find yourself in the same situation. Leverage investing can be a dream come true for you if you are careful to consider just a few things.

1. In the beginning, **avoid any properties that have a negative cash flow.** It is pretty easy to figure out whether a property has potential profitability or not. There are so many houses on the market that are being offered as great deals, yet they produce a negative cash flow, which means that you have to take extra money out of your pocket to pay the bills, over and beyond your rents. The income from your investment property needs to be able to pay all of your current borrowing cost, and also annual maintenance cost. So many people overlook maintenance, and that is definitely something that has to be figured in no way around it. This same concept applies to dividend paying stocks and also government bonds. The investment needs to pay for itself! If it doesn't it's not the right one for you.

2. **Don't put all your eggs in one basket.** This is pretty logical advice. When you put all of your investments in one area, particularly if you aren't familiar with that area, you will lose way too much if things go bad. When you have too much invested in one area, you don't have room to breathe and the smallest mishap can ruin you. I always say that you should stay within

the 5%–10% range. This means that you should not leverage an investment that would compromise five to ten percent of your net worth. Big investments deals require far more capital than smaller ones. And of course you make quite a big more profitability from the larger deals. My advice is to start small and learn as you grow in the process. Don't feel as if you need to become the next Donald Trump overnight, it took him years to get to where he is. I'm sure if we had a conversation he, too, would admit that he's lost a whole lot along the way. Remember, Donald Trump has more ability to survive a big loss than you do.

3. **Things Take Time!** No matter who you are, remember things take time. This book is not about getting rich quick. It's about getting an education through reading, applying what you have read, doing your research, and getting experience. Getting the knowledge and proficiency to become a big-time leverage investment guru is possible, but it will take time. Don't be in a hurry! People that rush too much usually miss out on the valuable lessons that they needed to learn along the way.

CHAPTER SUMMARY

- Get proper advice and avoid greed and ignorance.

- Regular monthly investing may not get you where you want to go.

- Don't over extend or over leverage yourself—leave a buffer.

9

REAL ESTATE INVESTING

For several years real estate investing has been a HUGE passion of mine, and also a significant part of my investing success. I would like to share my personal journey with you. As I've already stated in the chapter on leverage investing, I started when I was 14-years-young working at Wendy's. I was investing approximately $800.00 per month or $10,000.00 for the year. The market went up roughly 10% that year and I had $11,000.00 in savings. This worked well for me, but I really wanted to get further ahead so I started borrowing money to invest.

This method served me well too, but I still had to make monthly payments. So I began looking for an investment where someone else would make the payments for me. I did not really know if such a concept even existed, but I thought it was worth investigating. That's when I discovered real estate. At the time I had actually began selling real estate for a living but never really understood the investment part. The closer I looked, it began to dawn on me; I could buy a home for let's say $100,000.00, put $20,000.00 down and the tenant would pay off the remaining $80,000.00.

After that discovery I thought I was the smartest person in the world. If everyone knew this surely they would be doing the same, so I thought. I also learned that if the home value went up the tenant wasn't entitled to any gains; they were mine to keep (tax free, as I will explain later). Now I had a basic understanding and it made sense. Then I began to look at how real estate values tend to increase over time and found out that they are pretty stable; slow to rise and slow to fall. Depending on the areas, prices rose on average 3%-6% per year.

Some investors might look at these percentages and say that a 3%-6% annual increase in real estate values is hardly worth investing in. However, in the first year you buy a property for $100,000.00 (this may be a bit higher or lower depending on your area) and during that year the value of the home increased by 5% or $5,000.00, so at the start of the second year, your home is worth $105,000.00. So what was your rate of return? For some your answer may be 5% as the home was worth $100,000.00 and now is worth $105,000.00.

Let's look at it in a different way, you invested $20,000.00 and had a $5,000.00 increase in the value of your property. So the return on your money invested was actually 25% not 5%. This doesn't even take into account the mortgage payments that reduce a small amount of the principal owed on the property. Considering that, the actual rate of return is even higher. By this time I convinced myself that real estate was a viable investment. My next thing would be to find "the perfect property." Nearly eighteen months or so had passed and the "the perfect property" hadn't crossed my path.

Be Careful Who Gives You Advice

Maybe the perfect property didn't exist, I thought, so buying something was better than taking no action at all. I decided I would look at as many triplexes as I could get into on a Saturday and then buy the one that I thought was the best one out of the bunch. The next weekend I'd do the same with duplexes. Well this is exactly what I did. In the beginning I had no direction or clear criteria of the type of properties I should buy, but getting into the market was important for me.

The following weekend my co-worker who had been a respected businessperson for more than 30 years went with me to look at the properties. Thinking he would encourage me, he instead told me to "run away as fast as you can." This really got me down. I began to second-guess what I had done. The next morning after hardly sleeping at all I picked up the phone and called my co-worker. The conversation went almost exactly like this; we'll call this guy Dave.

> **Jeff**: Hi Dave this is Jeff, I just wanted to thank you again for looking at the properties with me yesterday, I respect you as a businessperson. May I ask how many investment properties you own?
>
> **Dave**: Jeff it was my pleasure, I was honored that you wanted my opinion. I actually don't currently own any.
>
> **Jeff**: Currently? So that means you have in the past, so what type of properties did you own?
>
> **Dave**: Actually I haven't ever owned real estate.
>
> **Jeff**: What about the home you are in?
>
> **Dave**: I rent.
>
> **Jeff**: Ok thanks again anyway for your time.

After hanging up the phone my mind was blank. This man was a respected businessperson who I assumed "had something." Why would I take advice from someone who never did what I was trying to do? That wouldn't make any sense! This experience taught me to dig deeper when someone tells me something by asking more questions and to try and seek advice from people that have done what I'm trying to do. Think about it for a second, if you needed brain surgery would you go and talk to someone that simply enjoyed heads and sharp knives?

You would probably consult a brain surgeon because of his or her experience. Why do we tend to listen to people about real estate investing that have never invested in real estate? Usually they are the only ones talking! As mentioned earlier, I attended monthly real estate investor meetings. Well I learned that real estate investors aren't out there bragging about the properties they own or going around trying to get others to invest, as if real estate investing is some sort of secret society. They tend to keep their business dealings ever so quiet.

 *Follow only qualified advice.*

Do you want to know the kind of person who does talk about real estate investing? It's usually your uncle Rick who knew a friend that had a cousin who knew a co-worker that had a brother whose sister bought a property and had nothing but problems. The tenants didn't pay and end up trashing the property. So there you go; you should never buy investment real estate. Are you getting my point? Find people who are success-ful in whatever field or endeavor you are thinking of investing your time and money into. Follow only qualified advice.

The Process of Growth

With real estate investing you can become financially free in a short amount of time. However, it will take work. People who want large amounts of money, yet want to invest no time always amaze me. Truth is, wealth building will take patience and effort, but it is rewarding. In 2002 I purchased my first triplex for $163,000.00. I purchased a fixer upper. Since the condition of this property was very poor. I knew that I would increase the value of the property and get really good tenants if I put some work into it.

After the purchase I spent approximately $15,000.00 fixing it up. The tenants that I found paid rents ranging from $700.00–$750.00 per month per unit. That was an increase of $750.00 a month in overall income. *(Please note—depending on your laws, you may have to have a vacant building in order to do this. If you have current tenants most States and Provinces in the U.S. and Canada have guidelines for rent increases each year. In my case I had a vacant building.) The next thing I did was order a property appraisal, it appraised for $259,000.00. When I purchased the house, I put 25% down payment, $40,750.00. My mortgage amount was $122,500.00.

With an appraised value at $259,000.00, I took out a new mortgage for $207,200.00, which meant I received a tax-free draft payable to me for $85,000.00. What would I do with the increase, buy a fancy car or take a luxury vacation? I decided to buy more real estate. With that $85,000.00 I purchased 3 Apartment style condo units in 2004. In 2006 I was able to re-finance these 3 condos and pull out $65,000.00 in equity. Now how was this possible in such a short period of time? I didn't have to spend a dime on renovating these units.

There were comparable units in the complex selling for more money. In a "single family unit" the way an appraiser determines value has nothing to do with the rent it brings in. Value is determined by comparing the home to similar homes that have recently sold in the area. In this case the complex had 108 units and they were all the same, give or take a few upgrades. The value of my unit was very close to the last 3-4 units sold. The last 3 sales were $110,000.00, which were approximately $25,000.00 more than I paid for mine.

When I purchased them for $85,000.00, I took out a $63,750.00 mortgage on each of them. Two years later they appraised at $110,000.00 and I took out an 80% mortgage at $88,000.00. This gave me approximately $65,000.00 after expenses and legal fees. With the $65,000.00 I purchased 2 more units. In 2007 I refinanced the original triplex and pulled out another $27,000.00 in equity and purchased another unit with these funds. The value of this triplex had only increased marginally since the last re-finance in 2004. The mortgage had been paid down which is why I was able to access $27,000.00.

Let's summarize this:

2002 Purchase of a Triplex for $163,000.00
2004 Refinanced and took out $85,000.00 in equity
2004 Purchase of 3 condominiums
2006 Refinance of 3 condominiums and took out $65,000.00
2006 Purchase of 2 condominiums
2007 Refinance on Triplex and got $28,000.00
2007 Purchase of a condominium

Why the detailed story? This is what is possible if you get in the game. It may or may not happen the same way for you, but it is possible!

What Type of Real Estate Should I Buy?

Before you move forward with buying property, you must answer this question. The answer to this depends on variable factors such as your financial situation and of course your goals.

But I can guide you in taking a couple of different approaches. Let's say you want to buy a multi-unit property, anything with more than 2 units. In this example, the property has 6 units and the sale price today is $600,000.00, and the rent is set at $6000.00 a month. With steady rent increases you should make out just fine. However, let's fast forward 10 years into the future.

What will things look like? Assuming that the rents hadn't been increased in 10 years, and you have maintained the property it would still be worth $600,000.00. If interest rates have increased your property value may have even decreased (if rates are higher the cash flow on the property goes down potentially making the value go down). This may seem like a stretch to think someone wouldn't increase rents, but it happens quite often. You see some investors don't want to upset or lose tenants. To a certain degree they may be right, but at what expense?

The lesson here is to make sure with this type of investment you increase the rents as they play a big role in determining the value of the property. These types of properties tend to require larger down payments than in my next example. My next example, I would be investing in a single-family unit. Today you purchase a single-family unit for $150,000.00 and fast forward 10 years to see what things might look like. Like the example above let's assume you didn't increase the rent the entire 10-year-period, what would things look like?

Well, the value may be $300,000.00 or $200,000.00, depending on the market. The rental income has no bearing on the value of the property. The buyer for this type of home is likely someone looking for a place to live in, not to invest. The market when you go to sell is anyone looking to purchase a home, whereas in the multiplex units you are primarily only looking for investors, which is a far smaller market for you to select from.

PROS and CONS for These Scenarios

Multi Unit buildings

Pros

• Generally have a higher cash flow
• 1 lawn, 1 roof, 1 property to maintain with multiple rental units

Cons

• Requires much more cash to get started
• Cannot liquidate a portion of your investment if needed

Single Family Units

Pros

• Possible higher price appreciation over time
• Can usually finance with less down payment
• Can liquidate one if needed without selling all your units

Cons

• Less cash flow
• Multiple places to maintain

One route is not necessarily better than the other. They are just different. These are only two examples. There are many different types of investments, such as land or commercial. I feel more comfortable giving you examples in my area of expertise.

Everyone has personal beliefs surrounding investing and wealth. In *The Millionaire Real Estate Investor* by Gary Keller, he mentioned a few beliefs about investing that I want to comment on to give you my perspective. Ultimately, you have to find out which one works best for you.

Dispelling the Myths

Myth #1

Myth: I don't need to be an investor—my job will take care of my financial wealth.

Truth: Yes, you do need to be an investor—your job is not your financial wealth.

Do you know someone who thought their job would take care of them forever and due to downsizing, the economy, or other reasons the job isn't there anymore? And very few people become financially wealthy from working a job.

Myth #2

Myth: I don't need or want to be financially wealthy—I'm happy with what I have.

Truth: You need to open your eyes—You do need and want to be financially wealthy.

Some of us are taught to think this way. Do you ever remember your mother saying just be happy with what you have? If you choose to live this way, your future will more than likely be defined by extremely limiting financial choices.

Myth #3

Myth: It doesn't matter if I want or need it—I just can't do it.

Truth: You can't predict what you can or can't do until you try.

There is no way for anyone to know what your financial potential is until you try.

Myth #4

Myth: Investing is complicated.

Truth: Investing is only as complicated as you make it.

When it comes down to it most things have some degree of difficulty, don't they? Did you learn to ride a bike your first time or did you give up because it was too complicated? Great investing can be learned if you take your time and follow proven models.

Myth #5

Myth: The best investments require knowledge most people don't have.

Truth: Your best investments will always be in areas you can or already understand.

The real nature of investing is always investing in things that you know and fully understand. Choose an area that you already know or one that greatly interests you and commit yourself to becoming an expert in it over time. In my opinion, investing in real estate is one of the easiest areas in which to acquire expert knowledge and understanding.

Myth #6

Myth: Investing is risky—I'll lose my money.

Truth: Investing, by definition, is not risky.

Risk is the concept that people BRING to investing. Great investors don't think of investing as risky. Rather it's about following sound investment principles and models, and taking the risk out of the game altogether.

Myth #7

Myth: Successful investors are able to time the market.

Truth: In successful investing the timing finds you.

Timing is all about being active! You must be in the game all the time. The best deals come from the best opportunities, and the best opportunities come fast.

Myth #8

Myth: All the good investments are taken.

Truth: Every market has its share of good investments.

The market will always have great investments if you look hard enough and are looking in the right places.

Build your Network!

Before you get started you must begin to build your network of professionals that will help guide and support your real estate investments. They include tradesmen and professionals such as: plumbers and electricians, inspectors, appraisers, insurance agents, roofers, masons, contractors, property managers, lawyers, lenders, real estate agents, mortgage brokers, other investors, accountants and mentors, and people in the business of doing what you are doing. I can't stress enough the importance of having this group of people. When searching look for referrals from other investors and find what works for them, since they have more than likely gone through the pain of finding the right people.

Always ask for references and actually call them to see what their experience was like. Please don't shop solely on price alone as the cheapest usually doesn't mean the best. Time is money in business and getting things done quickly and right is more important than saving a few bucks. If you truly want to treat this as a hands-off business, hire a property manager. A property manager will usually charge a percentage of gross rents collected. This can range from my experience from 4%-7% depending on the size of the property.

 *Make sure you are aware of everything up front.*

The property manager is in charge of finding tenants, dealing with issues when they come up, co-coordinating repairs, collecting rent and evictions, which happens in this business occasionally. Some may have fees for certain services over and above the percentage they collect. For example: the eviction process, if they have to go to court on your behalf they may charge additional fees. At times they may have to run advertising that goes above their standard agreement with you. Make sure you are aware of everything up front. It's best to have a contract in writing with your property manager to avoid any misunderstandings down the road.

One of my regrets is that I didn't hire a property manager from the start; as it has allowed me to focus on other things like playing with my kids or buying more property. Here is why you need a good network. One afternoon a couple came into my office who were renting a unit from me and handed me the keys saying they were moving out of the country. Tenants are supposed to give 60 days notice but it doesn't always go that way. That afternoon, I went to the unit and they decided to leave almost everything they owned which happened to be junk.

On top of that the walls needed to be painted, and the kitchen counter, carpets, and floor all needed to be replaced. Well I went into quick action. That night I emptied the unit. By the end of the weekend my contacts had the floor and carpet done, as well as the painting. By Sunday there was a For Rent sign on the lawn. I had new tenants six days later. Rather than getting down on myself I stayed focused on the long-term goals.

My wife came to a Real Estate Investment Class I did a few months ago. When she heard me tell this story she asked, "Why didn't I know about this?" I said, "I usually never talk about the negative side of things as there is no benefit. If I came home and told you this story would it have made your day better?" Deal with the negative but focus on the positive. Some of you may be reading this saying that it's fine for me because I have the funds to pay for the repairs but you need to prepare yourself the same way I did.

If you have access to $40,000.00 today for the purpose of investing in real estate my advice would be to use maybe $30,000.00. Save the other $10,000.00 as a contingency plan. Perhaps you are at the point where you think real estate is something that might work in your investment portfolio. Where do you go from here? The very first thing you should do is find out what you can afford. Speak with someone who specializes in arranging financing for investors. This will make a WORLD of difference in your investing career. People often come to me to invest and say their bank told them an amount when in fact they qualify for much more.

The problem almost every time is the person behind the desk at your local bank isn't an investor and doesn't specialize in investing. It may take you some time to find the right person but look until you do. I had clients recently come to me, that had each earned approximately $35,000.00 per year and had 8 months prior purchased a home through me. They were now at the point where they wanted to buy an investment property. Her father had agreed to lend them the 5% down that was required for the type of property they wanted to buy.

They had nothing in savings, he worked in an industry that was laying people off and had to borrow the down payment. My advice to them was to wait until they had more of a down payment and possibly more job security. You may ask why I talked them out of doing something right now, isn't real estate the way to go? It can be, but real estate must be done properly, in order to become profitable. Just because they qualified for the loan doesn't mean it's a good idea.

Here were my qualifying questions:

1) If the tenant didn't pay for 3 months would that affect you?

2) If when they left you had a $2000.00 repair bill how would that affect you?

3) If one of you lost your job for even 1 month, would that affect you negatively?

What if all 3 happened at the same time? They told me that it would likely sink them financially. My advice was to wait. Sometimes waiting is the best thing you can do, when you really want to start off right. Preparation is always key to making the right deals. Next you need to research different types of properties and develop criteria that you will focus on. This is very important and will lead to greater profits over time if you focus on a certain area. It isn't common to see an investor who owns student buildings and then triplexes, most successful investors stick to one area, not that you have to, they just do.

I often have people come to me that want to "partner" with someone to invest. Be very careful of partners. If you can do it alone most of the time I suggest you do. Here is a common partnership that I see. You will have one investor that has the money and the other investor who knows how to use a hammer. The person with the money feels safe with the laborer as he or she possesses knowledge that the investor doesn't have. In many cases the person with the money gives up 25%–50% of the profits to the other. I'm here to tell the investor that you can hire someone to do that work in most cases without giving up ownership or profits.

 *If you do partner with a friend just make sure you have a clear exit strategy from the start.*

Another scenario consists of friends who want to buy together. While this may seem like a great idea at first, you must realize that situations change. What happens when one friend gets married? Or one gets divorced? Or one needs money and wants to sell? Things may seem like they will last forever but lives change. If you do partner with a friend just make sure you have a clear exit strategy from the start.

Advice I will often give to friends is to each buy separate properties and just be there to support each other and help each other out when needed. You have all the benefits of a partnership with no downside. Believe it or not where I see partnerships succeed, it's usually when family is involved.

Partnerships can at times work well. Just do your homework and get an understanding from the start.

Flipping Properties

The last thing I'll discuss in this chapter is the concept of "FLIPPING". Flipping properties is when you purchase a property and quickly sell it at a higher price. You buy a property, fix it up, and then sell it for a profit. This is not an area that I focus a lot of time on with clients, especially new investors. Flipping properties is much more labor intensive than regular real estate investing. Don't get me wrong, you can make great money flipping properties but you have to keep flipping in order to see profits. There are no long-term benefits or equity building from flipping properties unless you take the profits and invest them somewhere.

 *Flipping properties is much more labor intensive than regular real estate investing.*

When I speak with investors that have been flipping for many years their biggest regret is that they didn't invest in real estate along the way and purchase properties to hold. Flipping can be a great way to generate cash BUT you need to know your numbers. Most first time flippers actually lose money because they under estimate the costs and the time it will take to complete the project. This is not a how-to guide on flipping properties, but rather some suggestions if you are considering it.

If you find a property that you think would make a good flip, contact a trusted real estate agent and ask what he thinks the top price would be if the property was fixed up. Then have a contractor go through the home with you and get a detailed quote on the cost for the improvements you want to do (ask your real estate advisor on what improvement will get the best return, no need to use Gold trim if we can get away with Silver). Then sit down and look at all the costs.

Make sure there is room for error, if your contractor quotes $35,000.00 and it turns out to be $45,000.00 and your estimated profit was only $10,000.00 to start with you will be in trouble. This doesn't always mean you have a bad contractor. On projects things can come up that weren't expected. What if you thought it would sell at $300,000.00 and it only sells for $290,000.00? What if you thought it would sell in one month and it takes four months, leaving you with three extra months of carrying costs? My point is that there is a lot to consider and from my experience flipping is not the best place for a first time investor to focus.

Stay focused on your long-term goals and the speed bumps that may happen along the way. Real estate is not a get rich quick thing. Knowing what I have put in place for the future it has allowed me to not have to invest at all anymore, and know the future is going to be okay. I can now use my income to help others and to buy me time off, rather than having to use those dollars for investing. I still invest, just not new money anymore. I'm not some hot shot with all kinds of money to invest in real estate. I play the game, follow the wealth building principles and play to win. You can do the same!

CHAPTER SUMMARY

- Buy an asset and get someone else to pay for it.

- Find your niche and stick to it.

- Get past the financial myths!

- Build your network.

- Take advice from real estate investors.

- Choose partners carefully.

10

TRAINING YOUR CHILDREN

Train a child in the way he should go, and when he is old he will not turn from it. The rich rule over the poor, and the borrower is servant to the lender.
—*Proverbs 22:6-7*

It is pretty interesting that this Bible scripture which talks about training a child in the way he should go is not talking about training him up in faith, but rather in the knowledge of how the rich rule over the poor. It clearly tells us the borrower is servant to the lender. From this it is plain to me that one of the most important things that you can teach your children, early on, is how money works. This is an important part of demonstrating good fathering skills. It is one thing to provide for your children, and that's a great thing.

But how important is it when you can actually train your child so well knowing and understanding all-important facets of money, lending, and investing, that you really don't have to worry about how they will get along in life. You can rest assured that everything will be fine with them, because you trained them well. Let's back up for a minute, perhaps to when you were a child. Did your parents train you to know how money works? Or was your childhood basically like all of the other average kids in the neighborhood?

There is nothing at all wrong with having a normal childhood, playing games, riding your bike outside, and playing hockey for your school. Those are all great things. But every child will grow up and become men and women, and unfortunately when they become adults, there's not always much time to prepare for the real world. The best time to prepare your child for the real world is now. You might say, "It's too early for all that stuff about money. A kids mind can't comprehend those concepts." I'd have to beg your pardon on that one.

 *How do you teach money? Make it fun and practical!*

A child's mind is most flexible and able to receive mass amounts of information, even more so than older adults, simply because they don't have anything crowding their mind, like work, pensions, taking care of family, and the other cares of daily life. Their minds are like sponges ready to receive new information. The earlier you teach them the better their financial futures will be since they would have already received perhaps some of the most valuable information about finances that they need to know. So how do you train children up in the way they should go, properly understanding money management? The answer to that is two-fold; make it fun and practical.

Monopoly Money and Success

Is it possible to become rich by playing the board game *Monopoly*? I don't know the answer to that, other than all things are possible. What I do know is that playing this game and other games like it, can give you a sense of understanding about how money works in the real world. *Cashflow* is another board game that was actually made for adults which teaches lessons on how investing works. The reason that I suggest games is because you have to use approaches that are fun and engaging in order to hold a child's attention. *Cashflow for Kids* is available for children.

Kids hate boredom. Actually I'm not so good with boredom. I like to be engaged in a learning experience. I know that for the kids, it helps them to retain the information better. So in training your child learn to create innovative ways of teaching your children about money. Even if you don't have a board game, you can use something as simply as a piece of paper and a pen, and illustrate money examples on paper. Kids love visuals, and they love spending quality time with their parents. So the very fact that you are actually showing them what to do on paper, will actually engage them.

One of the ways that has always been effective is to actually expose your child to what you do when you pay bills. Teach them how to balance a checkbook. Teach them how to write a check. Explain to them how you deposit money in your banking account and when you write a check the money comes from your bank account and goes into the account of the person that you are writing the check to. Tell them why you must keep good records of your spending. And ask them what kinds of things they would like to spend on when they get money.

Naturally most children are going to think about things that are on a child's level, but that's a good start. After they've given their wish list, then you can let them know that they can have those things if they have a way of paying for it. That's when you can ease them into how investments work, and how investments can grow. Instead of hiding your financials from your children, include them in the overall discussion about day-to-day expenses and how to satisfy those expenses. What needs to be paid first, second, third, or last? These lessons will last for a lifetime as you are laying the foundation for a strong financial future.

As I have said earlier that there are five basic things that you can do with money, there are actually six. However, I really didn't need to go into detail about the first, which is earning, since most adults know that they should earn money. At least I hope that adults understand this entry point to money. Earning is the most fundamental principal, which says that you give time, mind, or creativity in exchange for money. So let's look at each of these lessons, and discover how to help children understand these important lessons.

Earn

To teach this basic lesson you can give your child a job or assignment in which they will earn an allowance or even actual pay. I've always thought that you should give your child something to do that needs to be done that will help to free up your time. Perhaps emptying the trash on a daily basis and then putting the trash out for the garbage truck to pick up. This certainly has a cash value to it. Your child can wash dishes, or clean up the kitchen or bathrooms. Maybe they can wash your car, and the money that you'd normally pay a car wash, just pass it over to them. Kids can do a wonderful job mowing the lawn, and trimming the hedges, if they are old enough to know how to handle such equipment. They can have a paper route delivering newspapers or even pet sit for a neighbor. The point is getting them to understand that through their own creative ideas and actions, they can earn an honest wage.

Save

After they've earned money, now it's time to teach them how to save. You should teach them that they cannot spend everything that they earn otherwise they'll be left with nothing. They have to put a sizeable amount aside. As I said, I was able to save great amounts of money because I, like most children, had no expenses. Teach them that they are fortunate to not have expenses and that the day will come when they'll have expenses. So take advantage of the ability to save money now. I'd suggest that they save 60% of their money.

Spend

Money is something that needs to be enjoyed. So we don't want your child to save every dime and never have enough for snacks. Let them know that they can purchase some of things they want to buy. Let them feel the joy of spending money that they've earned. However, let them also know that they aren't to go overboard in this area, as this area is an area where most people fail to be disciplined and potentially ruin their financial futures. Perhaps 10%-15% should be set aside for spending.

Invest

The next lesson is that if you don't invest, you cannot expect to see more money coming in until you earn it. This is where you teach your children how to make money when you are sleeping. This is where your child will learn how money makes more money through investing it in the right area. Find investments that your child can participate in and get them started early. Begin investing at least 10%, even more if you can.

Lend

This is an area where you should teach your kids how lending money can be profitable. Teach them how the banking system works and how the banks get extremely rich from lending to people at interest rates. Teach them that they too can lend money just like the banks. But they should follow the same example of the bank in that they properly screen the people who want to borrow money. Never lend to anyone who doesn't have the means to pay back the loan. Never lend to someone who has a track record of not paying on time. Never lend to a person who already owes more than they can afford. Explain to them the good and bad, and teach them how lending without proper counsel can get them into big trouble. There is joy in lending, but only when you play by the rules of the game.

Give

This is the highest level of money management. What an important lesson to teach your child, that giving is the highest level there is. You must teach your child that the ultimate experience is when you have managed so well in this financial game that now you are able to give to every good work, all around the world, helping people everywhere. Here you can teach your child to give 10% of their income away to charity, a ministry, to help the poor and needy, or whatever good work they want to get involved in. This is the level where your money is circulating so fast that it is just waiting to come back to you. Teaching them to be givers will show them the great value of selfless living, doing everything possible to help all of humanity.

Growing Up

You may think that the Millionaire Father grew up in a wealthy neighborhood with rich parents, right? Not exactly. I grew up like most do in a middle class neighborhood in a loving family. My father was a schoolteacher and my mom was a homemaker. Growing up I really had no concept of rich or poor. What I knew was that my parents provided meals, warmth, and comfort. They went to every single basketball and baseball game I played in and would sometimes treat me to donuts after church or a gingerbread cookie at the farmer's market. Most of the things that I remember about being a kid didn't specifically involve money; it involved spending time with my family.

My parents had opposing views about money. My mom was the saver. She grew up on a farm with a large family. All her clothes and siblings' clothes were hand-me-downs; they rarely ever had anything new. They grew and raised their own food and went to the bathroom outside. I believe that her way of growing up led my mom to want something different for her family. So saving was a way of insuring that we would never go without. She would even start saving in January for next year's Christmas presents. So I adopted the habit of saving through watching my mother's example.

My dad, however, was the spender. He wasn't an over-spender by any means. He never had any real debt to speak of, but he had no savings either. He didn't think about the long-term future too much because he had low expectations. Both his grandfather and father died at a relatively early age. I suppose, given their medical history, he expected to die early as well. However, I am happy to report that at this writing he is happy and healthy at 58.

So, in short, I grew up in a home where my parents treated money very differently than most folks did.

I never saw them fight about money although I could sense they didn't see everything eye to eye. I likely have a little of both of them in me. Yet the most important thing for me is that I become the kind of example that I would like to see demonstrated in my boys' life when they become adults. What I do now, and how I view money, is going to play a large part on how they handle money. The point is that the first and most prominent example that your children will have of how money should be earned and properly used will come from you. So make it your priority to become as financially proficient as you can possibly become so that your children follow a solid example.

CHAPTER SUMMARY

- It is your responsibility to teach your children about money—if you don't who will?

- Make learning about money fun and practical.

- Expose your child to what you do financially.

11

MULTIPLE STREAMS OF INCOME

In a challenging economy people often seek out various ways to create wealth. My thought is that whether the economy is stable or ironclad, you should still seek out different ways to create wealth. The creation of wealth should not be based on your personal need alone. The creation of wealth should be based on purpose, and your purpose is based on your assignment in life. Usually your life's assignment will include more than just you and your family. So the more you focus on how you can help others, the more your territory, your exposure, and your wealth will expand.

It is my experience that money comes most regularly to the ones who have a specific assignment for its purpose. Do you have something for your money to do? Or do you view money as something to get just because you have a burning desire to go shopping? Honestly, you can only buy so much before whatever it is that you purchased begins to crowd your space. So then, your income will be based more upon what your plan is for it. Even if you just focus on your family, which isn't a negative thing, you will still find that just with your family and rearing children you have multiple needs for money, now and later.

Weddings, college tuitions, proms, graduations, and family vacations, are just a few of the longer term and possibly ongoing needs for money. Depending on how old your child is will determine how close you are to needing to pay for these things. Regardless, at some point various things will come up, and when they do, you want to be fully capable of satisfying your obligation. That is what being a Millionaire Father is all about. I'm not talking about raising an army of bratish children that you give them whatever they want. The ideal is that no child misses out on the things in life that he or she should have.

My ideal is that no child misses out on the things in life that he or she should have.

Your child and family will always have the pleasure of knowing and feeling a sense of great gratitude, that throughout life daddy was always prepared. Being prepared you must be a visionary. You must be able to intuitively know that times will change, as they always do. When the times do change you will be fully equipped for whatever change may come. Far too many people allowed themselves to be taken by total surprise, being laid off their jobs, or having their workplace suddenly go out of business.

In all humility I share with you that if I no longer sold real estate I would still be fine. The reason for this is simply because I prepared other ways to create wealth, so in the event one avenue shuts down, there are always many more open. I'm here to coach you on how not to be ever caught off guard again. Okay you've lost your job, your company folded, what are you going to do about it now? There is no sense complaining about what happened. What's happening now? I guess in the final scheme of things "what's happening now" is really all that matters.

I'd like to open your mind to a few ideas, each of which you can explore in greater detail later. I want you to become familiar with the whole idea of multiple streams of income. If you want to be wealthy in this era forget about working the same job for fifty years and then retiring rich. That's probably not going to happen. Is it possible? Anything is possible, but it is an extremely small chance. Those who make the most money today are those who in some way or another have multiple streams of income working for them. What I love most about this is that one area can fail, but all of the other streams of income keep moving forward like a mighty river.

 *I want you to become familiar with the whole idea of multiple streams of income.*

Rupert Murdoch is a billionaire who owns News Corporation. They have about $33 billion USD in revenue and about $5.38 billion in net income. Most people haven't heard of News Corp as they are called for short. But most people are very familiar with the many subsidiaries and businesses that they own such as Fox TV, Fox Broadcasting, 20th Century Fox, the Wall Street Journal, Direct TV, The New York Post, Harper Collins book publishers, Zondervan books, GQ and Vogue magazines, and MySpace both in North America and China.

Suppose Zondervan book publishers, the Christian book division of Harper Collins, went out of business, do you think that it would cause News Corp to go bankrupt? I can assure you it wouldn't. The reason is because they have so many streams feeding the corporation that money will continue to flow throughout all of its subsidiaries and businesses that it really wouldn't cause major damage to the everyday business of the company.

By the way, this is a very short list of their holdings. Now I realize that I am comparing YOU to a multi-billion corporation. That's on purpose. You should model your own finances after this pattern of creating more than one way to keep wealth flowing into your life. If something isn't working then you'll always have a backup ready to kick in. There are multiple types of businesses that you can easily get involved in. I have listed a few start-up businesses just to get your thoughts going, and hopefully provoking you to search even further from here discovering more things that you can do to create a positive cash flow.

Internet businesses

Since its inception the Internet has been one of the most booming businesses to ever hit the face of the earth. By the looks of it, it doesn't seem like it's going to slow down any time soon. The Internet has become for most PC and Mac owners globally, a way of life. Since there are already hundreds of millions of people who use the internet, perhaps even a billion or more, why not tap into an already built in audience just waiting for you to service them with your creativity.

The Internet has become for most PC and Mac owners globally, a way of life.

There are so many businesses that you can get started online. I'll just mention a few just to prime your interest. There is affiliate marketing which is when you help to promote other people's company, goods and services on your website. Whenever a sale is made you get a commission from that sale. Auction selling is the selling or products both new and used online through already in place businesses such as Amazon.com, Craigslist and eBay. You can recruit for companies and find them employees. Once they hire the person that you have matched with their company, you get paid.

You can be an online consultant to large and small corporations and other businesses, helping them to solve problems that you are an expert at solving. A really big area of growth is in the area of research, where you do research for large corporations, pharmaceutical companies, big-time law firms, and even for academics who just don't have the time to do the research. A virtual assistant is basically an administrative support to small businesses. They provide customer support and service on behalf of these companies by providing answers online and often over the phone.

Network marketing

Network marketing is a term used to describe the type of marketing that was once performed by the company, but now assigned to an individual to market the company's good and services throughout that person's own network or friends, family, and associates. The concept is very much like social networking, where you can influence and market to your friend through a network such as MySpace, Facebook, and LinkedIn. There are literally thousands of network marketing business opportunities to choose from.

Many of them provide excellent training and support on how to build your business, which is usually included in the small start-up cost for joining. You have to find the one that works best for you. In your spare time you can easily find a network marketing opportunity that aligns with your personal taste by searching the web, or visiting your local bookstore's magazine section and looking for magazines that specialize in network marketing and small business start-ups. However, be sure you fully investigate whatever company you are considering. You want to be sure that they'll still be around in the next five years and not just a fad

Home based businesses

There are so many home-based businesses that are available. The list is pretty exhaustive. Just to name a few profitable ones that I have seen, Medical Claims Billing, Legal Transcriptionist. Tutoring students in various subjects, personal fitness trainer, professional photography, catering, an events planner, home remodeling business, home inspection business, home and office cleaning services, child care services, and pet grooming services. There are so many more that I could add to this list. However, by now I am sure that you are getting ideas running through you about how you can create various streams of income by doing what you already love to do.

There are several advantages to having a home-based business. One major benefit of owning a home-based business is that it reduces your tax liability as you can deduct expenses related to running your business in the home. Before you start to go wild in this area of tax breaks, please consult an accountant who is knowledgeable in tax law to inform you on what you can and cannot do in your particular country. Another obvious advantage is that you never have to fight with the traffic as you get the high honor of being able to conduct daily business from the comforts of your own home.

Be Prepared!

It has always been in my heart to help people to understand how to create wealth and live the life they deserve. I especially love helping fathers who have a sincere desire to provide a first class lifestyle for their family. My goal is to show you how easy it is to have a continual flow of wealth. I have discovered that many people, certainly not all of them, who are experiencing financial hardships today, are there because they do not realize they have multiple options. You are never tied down to a dead end job or a career with a lid on it. You can create the lifestyle that you dream of, by simply doing a little research. It's really that easy.

My goal is to show you how easy it is to have a continual flow of wealth.

You are just moments away from tapping into the reservoir of your highest potential. Instead of worrying about how you are going to make it, do something as simple as this: go into a bookstore and just start reading various magazines in the business and entrepreneur sections. You will be amazed at how many businesses are just waiting for you to get involved. Many of them don't require much training at all, as the companies offering these packages have minimized all of the administrative and difficult part of running a business, so that you don't have to sweat the small stuff.

It's free to go to the bookstore and look at magazines. If you have it in your budget, I always recommend going to workshops or seminars where an expert will teach you how to increase your value by using proven techniques and strategies. If you aren't comfortable there, you can always go to your local library and research as well. Then if you are just the kind of person who really doesn't like to be seen in public, you can always stay home on your personal computer and surf until you find the right stream for you. The real difference between those that will always stay on top financially is one thing, not books smarts, not personal strength, not how many friends you have, but your ability to take action NOW!

Above all, please be smart about things. I see too many fathers start businesses that are initially successful. After four months they made more money than they were at their regular jobs, so they quit. Instead, they dedicate all their time to the business. However, their venture didn't continue to have a steady income, and before they knew it, it snowballed out of control, leaving them in financial shambles and their family broken. Financial strain on a marriage can cause a lot of damage. Make sure things are running smoothly for 1-2 years before you give up your day job for your family's sake.

CHAPTER SUMMARY

- Create multiple streams of income—if one stream dries up you'll have others to draw from.

- Don't count on the one stream you have right now to last forever.

12

KNOWING WHEN YOU'VE HAD ENOUGH

Tycoon John D. Rockefeller was asked the question, "How much money is enough?" He answered, "just a little bit more." This question has been asked many times before. But what if I asked you the same question, how much money would really be enough for you? The answer to this will vary from one person to the next. The very nature of money is to fulfill a particular job. Money is always on an assignment. Sometimes that assignment is very positive, other times the assignment is not empowering at all. What matters most, is that you understand that money only does what it is commanded to do, and you are the Chief Officer in command.

"How much money is enough?" ...just a bit more." —John D. Rockefeller

What assignment does your money have? Or how much money do you need to fulfill your life's assignment. Perhaps you've never thought about the answer to that question. The answer to this question is very important because once you've discovered your life's assignment then you can measure the amount of money that you will need in order to fulfill it. If you never discover your life's assignment, you will continue to chase money in life and find that you are never being fulfilled. I've seen parents do this; they will spend dozens of hours a week trying so hard to give their children an above average lifestyle.

There is nothing wrong with working hard long hours when it is necessary. But it doesn't have to be every day necessarily, every week, all month long, for the rest of your life. The money is good, but spending time with those you love is even better. As much as kids like cool things and fancy stuff, they actually desire far more to spend close time with their parents. They want that more than anything in the world. I could be booked all over North America speaking on various topics. Instead I choose to limit my travel time on the road, take selected speaking engagements, and spend time with my wife and two boys.

You are probably thinking, "You'd actually turn down all that money?" For sure I would. I understand when I have had enough. I have a primary dedication to my family. Next I realize that there are thousands of people out there who need my teaching, they need me as a coach. Finally, there are so many people who are not as fortunate as I am and they need me to help them in one way or another, through a financial gift, donating clothing, supplying food and shelter. Although I am not limited to these areas, they are a great part of my purpose in life.

So I measure the amount of money that I need based on that criteria. Once I have arrived at that point, the actualizing of my dreams, then I can enjoy it. I can also hold back from getting caught up in the madness of living my life in a vicious cycle of lusting after more without a clear objective in mind. Some people say, I want more just because, and I don't need a reason in particular to want more. Well I don't really agree with that train of thinking. That kind of thinking lands you in a situation where you will never taste satisfaction because your mind just can't learn to be content.

It's All Relative

To a homeless person you may be the richest person in your city. Why is this? It is because wealth is always relative. It is relative to your mission in life. Donald Trump, Bill Gates, and Warren Buffett all have wealth relative to their callings and profession in life. What they do necessitates their salaries; that's why few people in the world live at their level in life. But is it necessary to live at their heights just to be considered successful? There are so many people who live well, live wealthy, healthy, and whole who have far less zeros on their net worth report cards.

...wealth is always relative.
It is relative to your mission in life.

Mother Teresa, who was a pretty remarkable woman, didn't have the need for personal income that Gates would need in order to keep his empire soaring. They had two different assignments, and so the amount of money for each of their respective assignments showed up when the time was needed. I'm sure that Mother Teresa could ask for the support from many people of means and receive it, based on her commitment and dedication to her worthy cause of helping people to experience unconditional love.

So money is not relative to who you are but rather what you are supposed to do. Every person in the universe has intrinsic value and great worth. So money doesn't just show up just because you are a good person or a loving soul. Money comes to help humanity complete a mission already set in place. So after you have purchased the yachts, the fleet of cars, six closets full of designer clothes, then what? Where do you go from there? You see, I am the first to admit that I really enjoy nice things in life.

 *So money is not relative to who you are but rather what you are supposed to do.*

More than that, I love giving my family the best of everything that I can give them. But after I have done that, and I have satisfied their corporeal needs, do I still need more money to give to them on another level or do I need to know when enough is enough? Unless you place constraints on yourself you may wind up missing the whole point of money in life. At the end of the day you'll still be crying, "A little bit more, a little bit more." In all actuality after you have given on the level that is relative to your mission, your family, and especially your children don't want more money, or even the things that money can buy, they want more of YOU!

Money Gives You Freedom

What does money, or more money give a person? Let's get beyond the surface things like more material things, bigger houses, faster cars, and more expensive toys. Beyond the feeling that some people get by having more money, or even the sense of security that some people feel when they have money, what does money really give you? In a nutshell, money gives you freedom, and freedom is worth a lot. It's pretty clear that money gives you the freedom to do more, have more, and enjoy more. But more than that, money gives you the freedom to choose.

In a nutshell, money gives you freedom... the freedom to choose.

There is a saying the poor have no voice. Often that same phrase is connected with children as well, because neither group of people has access to their own money. Why do citizens of free nations play such a major role in government? Their voices are heard through petitions, written letters, marches, and even lobbying. There is one clear reason for this. All of these people are taxpayers, and tax dollars keep the government growing. They have money and because they do, the government is willing to listen to their concerns.

So then, another way of looking at when you have had enough, is to ask yourself the question, "What freedoms have you not experienced simply because you did not have enough money to enjoy it?" Whatever that freedom is, I encourage you to pursue it. Enjoy it! Live it up! This entire book is about you through the power of action and the knowledge of proper investing embracing a better life for you and your family. Don't mistake this chapter to mean that I am setting restrictions on you and your ability to create more and more wealth.

My objective is only to get you to realize that after you have set out to reach this great goal, that you will arrive there, and once you do, you need to rest for a moment and enjoy the fruits of your labor with your loved ones. That's all. I have seen people work two; three and more jobs to pay for the home they never got to enjoy because they were always working. They don't know what any of the rooms look like because they are always working hard to create an illusion of wealth. True wealth is not about having things but rather about being able to honestly and truly enjoy all that you have. Remember your family is a part of your more valuable asset.

Setting Up a Value System

Here is my take on this whole matter. I'm not telling you that you have to set a limit on how much money you should have. That is really up to you, your assignment in life, and what you believe you are supposed to have. For me, I know what I desire and as I reach that goal, then I use the free time to enjoy my kids and watch them grow (and boy do they grow fast). So if you want $1 million dollars, $25 billion dollars, or $75,000 that is up to you. My plea is that you begin to take a personal assessment of your life and based on your core beliefs, begin to set up a value system that works in agreement with those beliefs.

I know of a very famous professional athlete, whose net worth is in the hundreds of millions of dollars, even after he has been officially retired for several years now. He has several businesses that all produce a positive cash flow for him. He endorses several sports equipment, apparel, and even food products adding multiple millions of dollars to his already huge income. Through his own admission he has expressed that his relationship with his children has become almost non-existent as he spends more time outside of the home on business ventures than he does with his children.

His wife and him are divorcing because of this. Yet not too long ago he took on another position to coach a professional team for multiple millions more. If he never worked another day of his life, or if this man never took on another position, he would have enough money to take care of his assignment. Yet he wants more. There are times in life when your desire to have more, can turn into a form of greed. Greed, my friend, is never satisfied, doesn't care who it hurts, and will do anything to get— MORE.

Ok so you may not be that professional athlete but I bet many of you reading this can relate and maybe it's time to look in the mirror. Do you have enough right now? Could you downsize your home and fancy cars allowing you to spend more time at home than at the office?

 *Money doesn't change a person, it only exposes who they really are.*

Maybe you don't have to downsize at all, you just need to stop working so much. In my position I have seen lots of "successful" business people and many of them are failures in their personal lives and isn't that what really matters? At the end of the day do you want to be remembered for being a top salesperson (just an FYI, nobody will care but you) or do you want to be remembered as a great father, husband and community leader? I may sound like I'm coming across pretty strong but maybe I need to have you see life the way it was meant to be.

You may be thinking, "Jeff, I thought you said that money was relative to your mission. Suppose his mission requires him to have more and more money, then what? While I am no judge of human character, all I can say to that is there are some things that are a priority in life. Money, as good as it is, can be limited in some areas. There are some things that money can't do. Money can buy you better health, but cannot always save the terminally ill. Money can't make you a loving person if you aren't one already. Money doesn't change a person, it only exposes who they really are.

Money can't make a family. Some things are only established through creating values and principles that you live by. Early on I set guidelines about my marriage and how I would be fully involved in my children's life from birth through adulthood. Anything that will come in the way of me doing just that, then becomes counterproductive to my value system and I simply have to dismiss it. When you have set up a value system then everything that you do, and what you don't do, has to support that system. Your money only works to assist you in strengthening your value system.

 *Money is good for the good it can do.*

I can't tell you what to value or what not to. That's up to you. For me it's family. For others it may be something totally different. But whatever that thing is, your money will obey and support it wholeheartedly. After all, Money is good for the good that it can do! Do good, take time, and enjoy the process!

CHAPTER SUMMARY

- How much money is enough for you?

- What assignment does your money have?

- Money is good, but spending time with those you love is even better!

- Wealth is relative to your mission in life.

- Unless you place constraints on yourself you may wind up missing the whole point of money in your life.

- Money gives you freedom.

- Set up a value system.

- Money doesn't erase your character—it only enhances it.

- Money can't make a family.

ABOUT THE AUTHOR

Jeffrey M. Reitzel was a self-made multi-millionaire in his 20's using the strategies he teaches in this book, which allows him to focus on the things that are really important in life. He is a loving husband to Penny, a father to Joshua and Lucas and the son of Jim & Sharon Reitzel. His passions include being with his family, teaching others to succeed at a higher level in their business and personal lives, and serving his community. Jeffrey is co-owner and Broker of a Real Estate Brokerage, and Mortgage Brokerage. He is a Lecturer for the Financial Services Underwriting Program at Seneca College of Applied Arts & Technology and Conestoga College. He is a Motivational Speaker and a "Son Of A Nice Guy."

Jeffrey has been a Guest Speaker for The Canada Mortgage & Housing Corporation (CMHC), The Canadian Institution of Mortgage Brokers and Lenders (CIMBL, CAAMP), The Chamber of Commerce, various real estate, financial planning and mortgage brokerage companies. Jeffrey is also featured on *House Calls* a weekly TV show on Rogers Television. He hosts a monthly *Millionaire Real Estate Investor Workshop*, was interviewed for *Millionaire Mondays* by best selling authors Jay Papasan, Dave Jenks and Gary Keller (Coauthors of the *Millionaire Real Estate Investor*) and was voted best dressed by *Canadian Mortgage Professional (CMP) Magazine*.

For more information go to www.themillionairefather.com.